DEDICATION

To David and Aaron, Deborah and Joshua,
Nicky, Emma, and Jonah

ACKNOWLEDGMENTS

We would like to thank the W.K. Kellogg Foundation and the Health Promotion Program at Michigan State University for providing the funding that enabled us to develop the curriculum on which this book is based. We would also like to thank the Psychology Department at Michigan State University for their support, and Dr. Silvan Tomkins, who pioneered the study of human emotions.

Thanks to our publisher, Judy Galbraith, for conceiving the idea of translating our concepts specifically for children.

CONTENTS

HEY KIDS! BE SURE TO GIVE YOUR PARENTS AND TEACHERS THE INSIDE SCOOP!

Positive self-esteem is the single most important psychological skill we can develop in order to thrive in society. Having self-esteem means being proud of ourselves and experiencing that pride from within. Without self-esteem, kids doubt themselves, cave in to peer pressure, feel worthless or inferior, and may turn to drugs or alcohol as a crutch. With self-esteem, kids feel secure inside themselves, are more willing to take positive risks, are more likely to take responsibility for their actions, can cope with life's changes and challenges, and are resilient in the face of rejection, disappointment, failure, and defeat.

Self-esteem is *not* conceit, it's *not* arrogance, and it's *not* superiority. Unfortunately, it's often confused with all three (and also with narcissism, egotism, and disrespect), which has contributed to a "self-esteem backlash." You've probably seen the articles and heard the assertions that too much self-esteem is bad for kids. Nothing could be further from the truth. Indiscriminate praise, flattery, social promotion, and falsely inflated self-worth are bad for kids, but those aren't what self-esteem is about. Self-esteem is based on facts and truths, achievements and competencies. The more self-esteem kids have, and the stronger it is, the better equipped they are to make their way in the world.

Conceit, arrogance, and superiority aren't the result of genuine pride. They are the result of *contempt* for others. Pride grows out of enjoying ourselves, our accomplishments, our skills and abilities. It's not about diminishing anyone else.

Contempt often masquerades as pride, but it's a false pride. When we're contemptuous of others, we perceive them as being beneath us. Secretly, however, we feel *inferior* to others. Contempt allows us to rise above those feelings of inferiority temporarily, but in order to keep feeling this way, we must continually find someone else to feel superior to—someone else we can put down in order to stay on top.

We believe that contempt is a root cause of two great problems facing our schools (and our world) today: bullying and violence. Bullies who taunt, tease, and harass others aren't kids with positive self-esteem and genuine pride in themselves. They are kids who lack social skills and empathy and may have other serious problems, including parents or older siblings who bully them, deep-seated anger, jealousy of other people's success, and loneliness. In order to bully others, you must believe that their feelings, wants, and needs don't matter. You must feel contempt for them.

When contempt combines with feelings of powerlessness and shame, this may (and often does) escalate into violence. We've seen this in the school shootings that have shocked us so profoundly in recent years. The children and teens who wounded and killed their classmates and teachers weren't kids with positive self-esteem and genuine pride in themselves. Some were bullied, tormented, and humiliated by their peers; some were rejected, excluded, and ignored. For reasons we may never fully understand, these kids developed absolute contempt for others, coupled with a desire for vengeance. It wasn't just that other people's feelings, wants, and needs didn't matter. Their *lives* didn't matter.

Self-esteem isn't the culprit here. Rather, the *lack* of positive self-esteem may lead some kids to take inappropriate, hurtful, even desperate actions. When we help kids build self-esteem, we're not teaching them to diminish others, and we're certainly not teaching them to be contemptuous. We're teaching them to take pride in themselves, feel good about themselves when they do the right thing (and own responsibility when they don't), celebrate their achievements (both tangible and intangible), know what they stand for (and what they won't stand for), and strive to be their best inside and out. When kids have a solid grasp of their feelings and needs, when they trust their emotions and perceptions, when they have a realistic sense of their capabilities, and when they have personal power—they feel secure and confident inside themselves—there's no need to put other people down.

Self-esteem isn't something we're born with. It's something we learn, which means it can be taught. We believe that all children should be taught the skills of personal power and positive self-esteem at home and in the classroom, right along with reading, writing, and arithmetic. All of these "basics" work hand-in-hand.

Stick Up for Yourself! is based on a program originally developed for adults. Called "Affect and Self-Esteem," it is currently offered as an undergraduate course in the Psychology Department at Michigan State University. To create this book, we adapted the course materials so children ages 8–12 can learn them on their own.

We encourage you to read this book with your child or your students and talk together about the stories, concepts, and activities. (You might learn a few things yourself!) As a caring, concerned adult, you're in a perfect position to help kids build personal power and positive self-esteem. Treat them with respect. Encourage them to do their best—without expecting perfection. Allow them to make mistakes and take positive risks. Give them opportunities to make choices and decisions. Invite them to share their feelings, needs, and future dreams. Be someone they trust and can talk to about things that matter to them.

For teachers, counselors, and group leaders who want to go further, we have written a companion teacher's guide for use with students in grades 3–7. For more information about *A Teacher's Guide to Stick Up for Yourself!*, please turn to the back of this book or contact Free Spirit Publishing.

It's our hope that the ideas and tools presented here will one day be a regular part of the curriculum—that all kids will be taught to stick up for themselves in healthy, positive, meaningful ways. Please let us know how *Stick Up for Yourself!* works for you and the children in your care.

Gershen Kaufman, Lev Raphael, and Pamela Espeland

WHAT IT MEANS TO STICK UP FOR YOURSELF

TYLER is having a bad day at school. Kids are hassling him again—calling him names, making fun of him, trying to trip him when the teachers aren't looking. He tries to ignore them, but they won't stop. Sometimes he feels like punching them all—or running away and not coming back.

That night, Tyler's mom asks him how his day went.

"I HATE school!" he says. "I'm tired of getting picked on. I wish I could quit going to school."

"You know you can't quit," his mom says. "You need to start sticking up for yourself."

ASHLEY'S parents blame her for everything. Last night, her little brother broke a plate, and they yelled at *her!* "If you had cleared the table like you were supposed to...." "If you'd been watching him like you should...." "If you'd pay more attention, like we've told you before...." Blah blah blah. It makes her sick!

Later, Ashley meets her best friend in an Internet chat room and tells her about it.

"They blame me for stuff I don't even do!" she pounds out on her keyboard.

"Parents can be so clueless," her friend writes back. "Don't let them push you around anymore. Stick up for yourself!"

JOSE knows the rule about not talking in study hall. He's quietly doing his math, minding his own business, when Matthew kicks him under the table for no reason. All Jose says is "Quit it, man!" And he doesn't even say it loud—barely a whisper.

Right away, the teacher orders him—Jose—to stay after school! Jose tries to explain, but the teacher cuts him off with "Not another word out of you." Meanwhile, Matthew sits there with a big stupid grin on his face.

Over dinner, Jose tells his family about it.

"You broke a rule," his dad says. "But it doesn't sound like you did it on purpose. Your teacher wasn't fair. You need to stick up for yourself."

When Tyler's mom tells him to stick up for himself, what does that mean? Should he start hassling the kids who hassle him? Should he fight with them? Should he try to get back at them for making his life miserable?

When Ashley's friend tells her to stick up for herself, what does that mean? Should she talk back to her parents? Should she whack her little brother for getting her into trouble? Should she go to her room and slam the door as loud as she can?

When Jose's father tells him to stick up for himself, what does that mean? Should Jose keep talking after the teacher tells him to stop? Should he kick Matthew and hope he talks, too? Should he go to the principal and complain about the teacher?

Did anyone ever tell *you* to stick up for yourself? Maybe you were confused, too. When you don't know what it means to stick up for yourself, you end up doing things it *doesn't* mean.

- Sticking up for yourself doesn't mean getting back at someone else.

- It doesn't mean acting bossy, stuck-up, or rude.

- It doesn't mean saying and doing whatever you want, whenever you want.

Here's what it *does* mean:

- Sticking up for yourself means knowing who you are and what you stand for, and being true to yourself.

- It means knowing how to speak up for yourself, and doing so when it's the right thing to do. (Sometimes it isn't.)

- It means there's always someone on your side—*you.*

WHAT YOU NEED TO STICK UP FOR YOURSELF

If you want to make a painting, you need paints, a paintbrush, and something to paint on. If you want to write a book, you need an idea, something to write with and on, and time to write.

If you want to stick up for yourself, you need *personal power* and *positive self-esteem*.

This book tells you how to get personal power. An important part of personal power is getting to know yourself. *You can't stick up for yourself if you don't know who you are and what matters to you.*

This book also tells you how to get positive self-esteem. *You can't stick up for yourself if you don't like yourself and feel a real sense of pride in yourself.*

HOW TO MAKE THIS BOOK WORK FOR YOU

Do you know the story of *Alice in Wonderland?* If you do, maybe you remember "Drink Me" and "Eat Me." When Alice took a sip from a bottle labeled "Drink Me," she instantly got smaller. And when she took a bite from a cake labeled "Eat Me," she instantly got bigger.

Reading this book won't make you instantly able to stick up for yourself. Learning how takes time. It takes work. And it takes *wanting to change.*

We believe you can learn how to stick up for yourself. That's why we wrote this book for you. You'll discover many ideas here that aren't usually found in books for kids. But we believe kids can understand them and use them.

In fact, since writing the first edition of this book in 1990, we've received many letters from kids who have tried these ideas. Here's what some of them have said:

○   ○   ○

"This book really helped me with my feelings. I used to fight a lot with my friends until I read it. I wrote about my feelings and talked with an adult, like you said. It worked."

○   ○   ○

"This book really helped me because I'm the smallest in my fourth grade class and everyone picks on me or makes fun of me. Since I read this book, I can stick up for myself."

○   ○   ○

"During lunch, my friend knocked a glass of milk onto the floor and blamed me for it. He said, 'You made me do it.' But I didn't listen. I know I'm responsible only for my behavior."

○   ○   ○

"There's this boy at school who always used to tease me. Now he stays away from me because I know how to stick up for myself."

○   ○   ○

"My mom and I talked about the book while I was reading it. Now I'm making more choices for myself. I used to go to my friend's swimming pool and my mom would pick me up when she was ready. I didn't like having to leave before I was ready. We talked about it, and she said I could call her when I wanted to come home."

o   o   o

"I'm making better choices now. I don't just go along with other people anymore. Especially when I don't want to."

o   o   o

"The part about being responsible really helped me. Especially the part that said we can choose to keep our hands to ourselves, even though we get mad and feel like hitting someone. Last time my sister and I got into a fight, I went in my room and sat on my bed and punched my pillow. I also like the part that said we can choose to do our schoolwork and chores without being nagged or reminded. That really helped!"

o   o   o

"I play baseball and I'm not too good. I strike out and miss fly balls and I'm not even in the starting lineup. After reading this book, I can say, 'Hey, I did my best.' That goes for my school subjects and other sports, too."

o   o   o

If you want this book to work for you, try these tips:

* Don't just read it. DO it! Whenever you see a "Get Personal" box, take time to do the writing activity. You'll learn a lot about yourself.

* Use a special notebook or journal for your "Get Personal" writing. Jot down other thoughts you have while you're reading. Add stories from your life. Set personal power and self-esteem goals for yourself, and track your progress.

✱ Share this book with an adult you trust—someone
who cares about you and wants the best for you.
Talk about the ideas and how they relate to your life.

Please let us know how this book works for you. Write to
us and tell us if it helps you stick up for yourself. Write to
us and tell us if it doesn't. Here's where you can reach us:

Free Spirit Publishing Inc.
217 Fifth Avenue North, Suite 200
Minneapolis, MN 55401-1299
email: help4kids@freespirit.com
Web site: *www.freespirit.com*

We'd love to hear from you.

Best wishes,

Gershen Kaufman, Lev Raphael, and Pamela Espeland

HOW TO GET AND USE PERSONAL POWER

When you hear the words "personal power," what do you think they mean?

A. BEING STRONGER THAN OTHER PEOPLE?

B. BEING SMARTER THAN OTHER PEOPLE?

C. BEING BETTER THAN OTHER PEOPLE?

D. BEING ABLE TO MAKE OTHER PEOPLE DO WHAT YOU WANT?

E. HAVING MORE MONEY THAN OTHER PEOPLE?

F. BEING FAMOUS, LIKE A ROCK STAR, A MOVIE STAR, OR AN ATHLETE?

G. ALL OF THE ABOVE?

When we use the words "personal power," we don't mean any of those things. Personal power means *being secure and confident inside yourself.*

Anyone can have personal power. Even though you're "just a kid," *you* can have personal power. You can learn how to get it and use it. No matter how you feel right now, you can learn to feel secure and confident.

It will take time and practice. It may take courage to make changes in your life. But you can do it!

Like the year has four seasons, personal power has four parts. They are:

1. **Be responsible.**

2. **Make choices.**

3. **Get to know yourself.**

4. **Get and use power in your relationships and your life.**

BE RESPONSIBLE

 You are responsible for the kind of person you are and how you live your life.

Maybe it doesn't seem that way to you. How can you be responsible if adults are always telling you what to do?

A lot of kids wonder about this. They confuse "being responsible" with "being in charge" or "being the boss" of other people and things.

> **SARAH** is baby-sitting her little brother Jacob while their parents are visiting friends. Jacob wants to watch his favorite TV program. Sarah wants to watch her favorite TV program. Sarah tells Jacob, "Mom and Dad said I was responsible. You have to do what I say."

Sarah is using being responsible as an excuse to get her way. That's not what it means. And there's something else it doesn't mean: having control over everything that happens to you.

There are many things in your life you can't control. Like the weather. Where your family lives. What school you go to. How much homework your teacher gives you. Whether someone decides to be your friend. And how other people act or feel.

Fact: *You are responsible only for YOUR OWN behavior and YOUR OWN feelings.*

Be Responsible for Your Behavior

BRANDON and Jamile are playing a car racing video game at Brandon's house. Jamile keeps winning, and Brandon doesn't like that. It's his game, and he should be winning!

Suddenly Brandon grabs Jamile's controller and crashes his car on purpose.

"Hey!" Jamile says. "What did you do that for?"

"You're not supposed to win every game," Brandon answers. "You made me do it."

ALYSSA is going to her friend Tracy's house to play. She's putting on her coat and heading for the door.

"Have you finished cleaning your room?" her mom calls after her.

"I'll do it later," Alyssa promises.

"I'd like you to do it now," her mom says. "You can play with Tracy when you're done."

Alyssa gets really angry at her mom. She gets so angry that she runs to her room, picks up her favorite toy off the floor, throws it…and it breaks.

Tearfully, she gathers up the pieces and takes them to her mom. "Look what you made me do!" she sobs.

Sometimes other people say or do things we don't like. We get frustrated or angry. We do something to get back at them. And we think that what *we* do is *their* fault.

We are responsible only for our own behavior. Jamile didn't make Brandon crash his car. Alyssa's mom didn't make Alyssa break her favorite toy. Brandon and Alyssa are responsible for their own behavior.

MAX and Zachary aren't allowed to go to the store by themselves. It's three blocks away across two busy streets. Their father thinks they're too young and has told them not to go.

One day, Zachary talks Max into going to the store with him to buy some candy. When Max hesitates, Zachary says, "Don't be a baby. Dad will never find out."

Later, their father finds the candy wrappers in the trash.

"I've made it clear that you're not supposed to go to the store on your own," he says. "Why did you disobey me?"

"It was Zachary's idea," Max says. "He made me do it."

Sometimes we let other people talk us into things we know we shouldn't do. We think this makes us not responsible (or less responsible) for our actions. But Zachary didn't make Max disobey their father and go to the store. Max is responsible for his own behavior.

"Mo-om!" Tiffany shouts. "MEGAN ate the last taco!"

"That was supposed to be Tiffany's," their mom scolds Megan. "I bought three tacos for each of you, like always."

"But I didn't mean to eat it!" Megan answers.

Sometimes we do things just because we feel like it. We don't think about what might happen next or how our actions will affect other people. But saying we didn't mean it doesn't undo what we did. Megan is responsible for her own behavior.

Kids aren't the only ones who get mixed up about this. There are plenty of adults who don't take responsibility for their behavior. Maybe you've heard some adults say things like, "I'm sorry I yelled at you. But you made me so angry that I couldn't help myself." Or "I'm in a bad mood, and it's your fault for arguing with me." Or "I didn't mean to miss your softball game. I had to go to a meeting after work."

Adults may use different words than kids, but what they're saying is the same: "I'm not responsible for my own behavior." Now you know this isn't true. So the next time an adult says, "You made me do it!" you can think to yourself, "I didn't make you do anything. I'm responsible only for my own behavior." This is a way to stick up for yourself.

IMPORTANT: Don't *say* it out loud. Just *think* it. Saying it will probably get you into trouble, plus it's rude. It's enough to know inside yourself that you didn't make the adult behave in a certain way. If you want, you can wait until things calm down, then ask the adult if you can talk about what happened. Work together on a plan for the future.

When we know—*really know*—that we're responsible for our own behavior, we can start making some important choices for ourselves.

✳ We can choose to tell the truth and not lie, exaggerate, make things up, or make excuses.

✳ We can choose to be trustworthy and reliable.

✳ We can choose to keep our hands to ourselves, even when we get mad and feel like hitting someone.

✳ We can choose to do our schoolwork and our chores without being reminded or nagged.

Being responsible usually makes good things happen at home and in school. The more responsible we are, the more people trust us, and the more freedom and privileges we get.

But this isn't the main reason to start being responsible. The main reason is because it's the best thing to do for you. Being responsible helps you feel secure and confident inside yourself. It gives you a feeling of *personal power.*

Here's something else you should know: Being responsible isn't the same as being perfect. You still make mistakes. You sometimes do things you're not supposed to do. Nobody's perfect! The point is, when you *do* goof up, you accept responsibility. You admit what you did and apologize. If you break something, you offer to fix it or replace it. If you take something that doesn't belong to you, you give it back. You do what you can to make things right. And if nothing you do seems to help, you move on.

Be Responsible for Your Feelings

Someone else can't make you grab another person's video game controller, break your favorite toy, or disobey your parents. In the same way, no one can make you feel happy or unhappy, excited or angry, bored or curious, or any other way. *You are responsible for your own feelings.*

But sometimes things other people say or do can act as triggers for our feelings.

"Did you put your bike away when you got home from school?" TONY'S dad asks him.

"Not yet," Tony answers absent-mindedly. He's busy drawing a new character for his comic book. Tony wants to be a comic book artist when he grows up, and he loves to draw.

"You never do it when you're sup- posed to!" his dad yells. "I want you to put your bike away RIGHT NOW!"

Suddenly Tony feels hurt and angry. Why does his dad have to yell? It seems like he always yells! He always accuses Tony of not doing his chores on time! His dad's words and yelling trigger Tony's hurt, angry feelings.

But maybe Tony often needs reminding to do his chores. Maybe he's in the habit of doing other things first or instead—like drawing. So when he says "Not yet," this trig- gers frustrated, angry feelings in his dad.

We can learn to ignore triggers and decide for ourselves how we want to feel.

MAKE CHOICES

fact: *Because you are responsible for your own behavior and feelings, you can make choices about them.*

You can choose how to act. You can choose not to grab a friend's video game controller or break a toy or disobey your parents. Even if you feel like doing these things. Even if the feeling seems overpowering or irresistible.

Many times, our actions are tied to our feelings. We hit someone because we feel angry. We yell at someone because we feel frustrated. We cry because we feel sad.

You can choose how angry, frustrated, or sad to feel. You can even choose to have different, more positive and productive feelings.

> **MARIA** studied hard for her math test, and she felt sure after the test that she had done well. But when the teacher handed the tests back, Maria saw that she had gotten six problems wrong. Her teacher had written across the top in big red letters, "You can do better!"

Maria has choices about how to feel. She can feel angry at her teacher for not seeing how hard she studied. She can feel angry at herself for not doing better on the test. She can think, "If I were smarter, I wouldn't get so many wrong. I must be pretty stupid." OR she can tell herself, "I did the best I could on this test, and what I did is good enough. I'll get help before the next test and try to do better."

DANIEL comes home from school excited to tell his mom about his day. His team won at volleyball...he had a fun band lesson...he finished his homework in study period...everything went great! But when he rushes in the door, his mom is on the telephone. She signals him to be quiet until she's through talking.

Daniel has choices about how to feel. He can feel rejected. He can think, "The person on the phone must be more important than I am. Otherwise Mom would hang up right away and pay attention to me." OR he can tell himself, "Mom probably won't be on the phone for very long. I can wait. I can listen to music while I wait so the time will go faster."

CARLOS loves his cat. He raised it from the time it was a kitten. It sleeps in his bed at night and walks with him to the school bus every day. When Carlos comes home after school, his cat is always waiting at the door to greet him.

One day, the cat gets very sick. Carlos's dad takes it to the veterinarian. The vet doesn't think the cat will ever get well. He thinks the cat might die soon.

It's normal and natural to feel sadness and grief at times like these. When someone or something we love seems about to die or be taken away from us, we can feel lonely and scared.

Still, Carlos has choices. He can choose to feel sad and worried all alone. OR he can choose to share his feelings with his dad. Together, they can talk about Carlos's cat and why it means so much to him. This might not make Carlos feel happy, but he'll probably feel less sad and worried. It helps to have someone we can talk to during hard times—someone who will listen to us and understand our feelings.

You can choose how to handle what life hands you. You can choose how you will face life's problems. This sounds like a lot for someone who's "just a kid." But we believe that everyone can learn to do it.

Expectations and Reality

An important part of learning to make choices is learning to make good choices. This starts with trying to predict what we *expect* will happen because of our choice, then deciding if our expectations are *realistic*.

In other words: What do we *want* to happen because of our choice? What are the chances it *will* happen? If the chances are good, our choice is realistic. If the chances are terrible, our choice is not realistic.

ANDREA has signed up to play basketball in after-school sports. She plans to practice every day and not miss a single game. She expects that by the end of the year, she'll be the very best basketball player in the school—maybe even the whole league!

It's great that Andrea wants to play basketball. It's great that she plans to practice and go to all the games. But when

Andrea expects that she'll be the *very best* basketball player, she's not being realistic.

Maybe she'll be a good basketball player. She might even be a great basketball player. It depends on how hard she practices, how often she gets to play, and whether she has a talent for basketball. But will she be the *very best* basketball player? The chances aren't very good. There can be only one very best, and there are lots of other kids in the league.

We live in a culture that values success more than almost anything else. It's important to be the best, the strongest, the fastest, the richest, the most popular, the best-looking, the biggest star. But that's not what personal power means. It means *doing our personal best at the things we believe are important.* And it means *liking ourselves even if our best isn't THE best.*

What are some realistic expectations Andrea can have instead? She can expect to learn a lot about basketball. She can expect to get better at dribbling, shooting, and playing different positions. She can expect that it will take time to learn these new skills. She can expect to have fun learning and playing. She can expect to make new friends on the team. Most important, she can expect to make mistakes instead of thinking she has to be perfect. These are all realistic expectations.

KAI'S family has just moved to a new town, and this is Kai's first day at his new school. At first, he feels anxious and afraid. What if the other kids don't like him? What if he gets lost or does something embarrassing? What if he doesn't fit in?

By the end of the day, Kai feels much better. Another boy, Emilio, has been nice to him all day.

Emilio showed him where the lunchroom was and where to buy milk. He invited Kai to play kickball with him at recess and introduced him to other kids at lunch and on the playground.

That night, Kai tells his family about his day. "I like my new school a lot!" he says. "A boy named Emilio was really nice to me. I think he's going to be my best friend!"

It's great that Kai feels excited about his new school. It's great that he wants to be friends with Emilio. But when Kai expects Emilio to be his *best* friend, he's not being realistic.

Maybe Emilio already has a best friend. Maybe Emilio was nice to Kai because the teacher told him to be. Maybe Kai and Emilio don't have that much in common after all. Or maybe they do, and they will become good friends. Who knows? Right now is too soon to decide.

Almost everyone has a hard time being realistic about relationships. This includes adults. We expect other people to care about us because we care about them. We forget that we can't control how they behave and how they feel.

What are some realistic expectations Kai can have instead? If he's a friendly person, he can expect to make friends at his new school. He can expect that it will take time to decide which kids he likes and respects. He can expect that it will take time for them to decide how they feel about him. Some might want to be friends with him—even best friends. These are all realistic expectations.

GET TO KNOW YOURSELF

KATE works hard to fit in with the popular clique at school. She tries to like the same things they like. She tries to hate the same things they hate. She bugs her parents to buy her the same clothes. She spends her allowance on the same music. She wears her hair the same way. She uses the same slang words. And on and on.

It's hard to keep up. Sometimes Kate wishes she could just be herself.

MARCO really wants to play soccer. He enjoys watching soccer games on TV. Over and over, he imagines himself actually becoming a soccer player. He feels very excited about it, and he thinks he would be good at soccer. Becoming a soccer player is a future dream for Marco.

But when sports sign-up time comes, his dad has a different idea.

"Guess what!" his dad says. "I'm going to coach a softball team this year! You'll be on my team. We'll have a great time together!"

Marco doesn't know if he should do what he wants or what his dad wants. Finally, he decides to go along with his dad. He plays softball instead of soccer.

Maybe you know people like Kate and Marco. Maybe you're thinking, "They should stick up for themselves!" And you're right.

If you work too hard to please other people, it's hard to get to know yourself. And this makes it hard to stick up for yourself. But you can make a change. A good place to start is by *naming and claiming* your feelings, future dreams, and needs.

Name Your Feelings

Back when you were learning to talk, you only knew a few words and sounds you thought were words. So you had to use the same word or sound to name many things.

Maybe you said "wah-wah" when you meant water—and milk, and juice, and all of the other things you liked to drink. When you said "wah-wah" to your mom, she had to guess what you really wanted.

Later, as you learned more words, you could be more specific. You could say "milk" when you wanted milk, "juice" when you wanted juice. From there you learned to say "apple juice" and "orange juice." You made an important discovery: The more *names* of things you knew, the more you could ask for what you wanted—and the more likely you were to get it.

Feelings have their own special names. The more names you know, the more you can understand your feelings and tell other people about them. And the more you can stick up for yourself.

Names are like handles for our feelings. Knowing the right name for a feeling allows us to "pick it up," learn about it, and make choices about it.

Calling feelings by their right names adds to your personal power. Calling feelings by their wrong names takes away from your personal power.

ZOE is lying on her bed with her blanket over her head. She just had the worst day of her life. Her best friend ignored her. Her teacher scolded her for not paying attention in class. A boy she likes found out that she likes him and now everyone knows. Plus she totally spaced out after school and forgot to stay for a Helping Hands club meeting. And she's the president of the club!

Zoe's dad walks by her room and sees her lying there. "What's wrong?" he asks. "Are you okay?"

"No, I'm not okay," Zoe sighs from under her blanket. "I'm really, really sad."

"That's silly," her dad answers. "Ten-year-olds don't have anything to be really, really sad about. You're probably just tired."

If Zoe goes along with what her dad tells her, she may learn to call her feeling by the wrong name. Whenever she feels sad, she'll think or say, "I'm just tired." She'll lose the handle for her feeling.

JEROME is having a problem about his older sister, Jada. It seems like their mom is always thinking of her first. *Jada* takes gymnastics lessons, so Jerome stays home and baby-sits their brother. *Jada* has the starring role in the school play, so Jerome has to do some of her chores for a whole month. *Jada* earns straight A's, but Jerome brings home B's and C's. *Jada* gets all the attention!

His mom can tell there's something bothering Jerome. "What's up with you lately?" she asks him one day.

"If you really want to know...sometimes it seems like the only person you care about is Jada," he says. "I guess I'm kind of jealous."

"It's not nice to be jealous of your sister," his mom says. "Jealousy is a bad feeling."

If Jerome goes along with what his mom says, he may learn to feel shamed by his jealousy. He may begin to deny his jealousy or lock it up inside of himself.

Feelings aren't wrong or right, bad or good. *Feelings just are.* When you know and accept this basic fact, you can start claiming all of your feelings. If you think you feel sad, that's how you feel. If you think you feel jealous, that's how you feel. Nobody can make you feel a different way. Nobody knows more about your feelings than you do.

Grow a Feelings Vocabulary

How good are you at naming your feelings? Is it easy or hard for you to come up with the right words to describe how you feel?

You can grow a feelings vocabulary by:

- listening to other people talk about their feelings

- asking for help explaining your feelings, and

- reading about feelings, the way you're doing now.

Dr. Silvan Tomkins was a psychologist who spent much of his life studying people's feelings. He believed that most feelings can be grouped into nine basic types. The first seven types include both a *low-intensity feeling* and a *high-intensity feeling*. The high-intensity feeling is stronger.

Here are the nine types of feelings Dr. Tomkins named:

LOW–INTENSITY	HIGH–INTENSITY
1. Interest	Excitement
2. Enjoyment	Joy
3. Surprise	Startle
4. Fear	Terror
5. Distress	Anguish
6. Anger	Rage
7. Shame	Humiliation
8. Dissmell*	
9. Disgust	

*Don't worry—we'll explain this strange word later.

Interest

When you're *interested* in something, you're curious about it. It holds your attention. You concentrate on it. You want to know more about it. When you're interested in a person, you're fascinated by him or her. Things (and people) you might be interested in are:

- a video game

- a TV program

- a good book

- a conversation you're overhearing

- learning something new at school or on your own

- someone who's a role model for you

- a new friend

GET PERSONAL
Write about at least three things or people you're interested in.

More names for interested: curious, fascinated, enthusiastic, passionate, concerned
Opposites: bored, uninterested, indifferent

Excitement

When you're *excited* about something, it's hard to think about anything else. Excitement quickens your pace; you walk faster and even *think* faster. Things you might be excited about are:

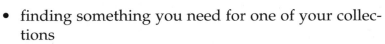

- going on vacation

- meeting new people

- your birthday

- taking a positive risk

- finding something you need for one of your collections

GET PERSONAL
Write about at least three things you get excited about.

More names for excited: thrilled, eager, happy, exhilarated, enthusiastic

Opposites: sleepy, bored, apathetic, dull, blah, couldn't care less

Enjoyment

When you're *enjoying* yourself, you're smiling and feeling good. Times you might be enjoying yourself are when:

- you're playing quietly with a friend

- your mom or dad is reading you to sleep

- you're petting your cat or dog

- you're relaxing with a hobby

- you're watching your favorite video

GET PERSONAL

Write about at least three things you enjoy doing.

More names for enjoying yourself: pleased, relaxed, satisfied, contented
Opposites: unhappy, tense, exhausted

Joy

When you're *joyful,* your whole body is full of happiness. You feel bubbly inside. The world seems like a wonderful place. Times you might be joyful are when:

- it's your birthday and you get all the presents you wanted

- you win first place in the chess tournament

- you fly on an airplane to visit your grandparents

- someone you like finally notices you

- you run a race from start to finish

GET PERSONAL

Write about a time when you felt joyful.

More names for joyful: glad, ecstatic, walking on air, flying high, lighthearted
Opposites: unhappy, down, sad, lonely, blue

Surprise

When you're *surprised* by something, you may not know how to act at first. You weren't expecting what happened, so you're not sure what to do. Maybe you don't say or do anything for a moment or two. You need time to process the experience. Things that might surprise you are:

- getting a letter or email from a friend who moved away a long time ago

- learning that your teacher went to school with your mom

- the first snowfall of the season

- an unexpected gift

- a compliment from someone you respect

GET PERSONAL
Write about a time when you felt surprised.

More names for surprised: amazed, astonished, impressed, blown away
Opposites: bored, blasé, indifferent, ho-hum

Startle

When you're *startled* by something—like a sudden CRASH nearby—your first response is shock. Things that might startle you are:

- someone jumps out at you from behind a tree

- you step off a curb into a puddle of icy water

- you sit down on a chair and find out—too late!—that it doesn't have a bottom

- a dog barks right behind you

- a scary scene in a movie or TV program

More names for startled: jolted, shocked, astonished, alarmed
Opposites: calm, settled, reassured, peaceful

Fear

When you're *fearful,* you're worried and afraid. You think something bad is about to happen, or someone is about to threaten or hurt you. Things that can make you fearful are:

- being alone in the house

- your first day at a new school

- thinking about tomorrow's math test

- hearing that a big storm is coming

- being bullied

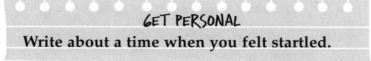

GET PERSONAL
Write about at least three things that make you fearful.

More names for fearful: scared, frightened, worried, nervous
Opposites: confident, brave, fearless, trusting, hopeful

Terror

When you're *terrified*, you're *very* frightened. You may feel paralyzed with fear—as if you can't move, even to help yourself. Things that can terrify you are:

- a nightmare

- getting lost or separated from your family in a strange place

- being chased by people who want to hurt you

- being in a car that's about to crash

- being in a disaster, like a hurricane or an earthquake

GET PERSONAL
Write about a time when you felt terrified.
Tell what happened and what you did.

More names for terrified: frightened, petrified, in a panic
Opposites: relaxed, encouraged, courageous, calm

Distress

When you're *distressed* about something, you feel sad about it, and sometimes you cry. Things that might distress you are:

- hearing your parents argue

- when your best friend moves away

- finding out that someone you love is sick

- being punished unfairly

- losing or breaking something you care about very much

More names for distressed: worried, upset, sad, tearful, crying, sobbing
Opposites: relieved, comforted, cheerful, glad

Anguish

When you're *anguished* about something, you're in *very great* distress. Other words for anguish are agony, misery, suffering, and despair. This is a strong and painful feeling. Things you might feel anguished about are:

- the death of someone you love

- knowing that something you did or said has hurt another person very badly

- believing you've just lost your best friend

- learning that your parents are going to get divorced

- learning about the problems of other people in the world—hunger, war, homelessness

More names for anguished: suffering, tormented, grieving, tortured, heartbroken
Opposites: reassured, safe, soothed, protected

Anger

Anger can be sudden and fierce, here in a moment and gone in a flash. Or it can start slowly and build, then burn for a long time. You might feel *angry* at a particular person or about a particular thing. Or you might feel angry at everyone and everything.

Some people confuse anger with feeling powerful. Because anger is such a strong feeling, they think it makes them strong. Remember that personal power means *being secure and confident inside yourself.*

Times you might feel angry are when:

- your sister reads your diary without asking

- you don't get your way

- a teacher says you were cheating when you weren't

- a friend breaks a promise to you

- your parents ground you for breaking a rule

More names for angry: mad, bitter, irritated, indignant, resentful

Opposites: loving, friendly, peaceful, agreeable

Rage

Rage is anger that boils over and blows up. Or it stays hidden inside, waiting to boil over and blow up, like a volcano. To feel *enraged* is to feel out of control. Times you might feel enraged are when:

- someone shames or humiliates you by insulting you, beating you up, or making fun of you

- someone takes something that belongs to you and won't give it back

- someone spreads lies about you

- someone treats you unfairly

- your parents change the rules and you feel powerless

GET PERSONAL

**Write about a time when you felt enraged.
Tell what happened and what you did.**

More names for enraged: furious, boiling, seeing red
Opposites: calm, quiet, soothed

Shame

When you're *shamed,* you feel exposed. You want to run and hide or cover yourself up. It feels like everyone suddenly knows you're just no good. Or like something is wrong with you inside, and everyone can see it. Times you might feel shamed are when:

- you ask someone for help and that person says, "Go away, don't bother me"

- your parents scold you for crying, saying, "Stop being a baby!"

- you have to give a speech in front of your class and suddenly your mind goes blank

- you want to approach some-one you don't know, but you feel tongue-tied

- you trip or fall and everyone around laughs at you

GET PERSONAL

Write about a time when you felt shamed. Tell what happened and what you did. Have you ever told anyone else about this? Think about telling an adult—someone you trust and can talk to.

More names for shamed: exposed, discouraged, uncomfortable, embarrassed, shy, guilty, self-conscious, inferior
Opposites: confident, proud, on top of the world

Humiliation

When you're *humiliated*, you're deeply and publicly shamed. You feel completely defeated by someone or something. You wonder if you can ever show your face again. Times you might feel humiliated are when:

- you forget your lines in the school play on opening night

- someone you trust tells other people a secret about you

- a parent scolds you in front of your friends

- another kid beats you up at school

- the kids at school start calling you a terrible nickname

GET PERSONAL

Write about a time when you felt humiliated. Tell what happened and what you did. Have you ever told anyone else about this? Think about telling an adult—someone you trust and can talk to.

More names for humiliated: mortified, disgraced, defeated, alienated
Opposites: proud, elated, self-assured

Dissmell

"Dissmell" is a funny-sounding word you've probably never heard before. (A lot of people haven't heard it, and it's not even in the dictionary, so you're not alone.) Dr. Silvan

Tomkins invented it to describe a specific feeling that didn't have a word. He wanted a word similar to "disgust," so he came up with "dissmell."

When you *experience dissmell*, it's usually because something or someone close to you suddenly smells very bad and you have to pull away quickly. Dissmell is our natural response to bad odors. First, your upper lip raises up on both sides of your face. Then your whole face pulls back, lifting your nose away from the nasty smell. You might wrinkle your nose and say something out loud, like "Yuck!" "Stinky!" "Smelly!" "P.U.!" "Gross!"

Go to a mirror and try to make your face look like this: Raise your upper lip and pull your face back. Wrinkle your nose. Then notice how you feel when your face looks like this.

Because dissmell shows so clearly on your face, the people around you can tell when you feel it. They might wonder, "Is it me?" and feel as if you're trying to push them away.

Times you might experience dissmell are when:

- you're walking down the street and suddenly step in dog poop

- you open the refrigerator, looking for something to eat, and smell something spoiled

- you come close to your baby brother and realize his diaper needs changing

- you're watching a movie and one of the characters falls into a garbage dump

GET PERSONAL
Write about a time when you experienced dissmell. Tell what happened and what you did.

More names for the feeling of dissmell: repulsed, repelled, grossed out
Opposites: attracted, accepting, welcoming

Disgust

When you're *disgusted* with someone, you can hardly stand to be around that person. You feel as if that person makes you sick. You feel like getting rid of that person, the way you would spit something out. It's also possible to feel disgusted with yourself.

Times you might feel disgusted are when:

- you discover that a friend has lied to you

- you realize that your parents aren't perfect

- you feel too grown-up for "little kid" stuff

- you stop liking someone and you don't want to be around that person anymore

- you do or say something you wish you could take back, but it's too late

GET PERSONAL
Write about a time when you felt disgusted with another person. Tell what happened and what you did. Then write about a time when you felt disgusted with yourself.

More names for disgusted: revolted, repelled, put off by
Opposites: affectionate, fond of, impressed

Combined Feelings

Did you used to think that being surprised and startled were the same? Or that being fearful and terrified were the same? Now you know they're different and each feeling has its own name. You're growing a feelings vocabulary and getting to know yourself better.

Sometimes it can be hard to tell feelings apart. That's because you can have more than one feeling at a time. Or you can have many feelings in a row, coming so quickly they all seem to mix together.

✱ You might feel *startled* first, then *angry* right after. Like the time when someone jumped out at you and scared you. You wanted to punch that person!

STARTLED   ANGRY

✻ You might be *enjoying* yourself when someone says something rude to you, and all at once you feel *humiliated*. For example, you're looking through a box of toys when you discover your old blocks. You take them out and build a tower—it's fun! Then your big sister comes into your room and says, "Look at the little baby playing with blocks! Isn't that cute!"

✻ You might go from being *surprised* to being *joyful*. Like the time your parents threw a surprise birthday party for you, or bought you a present you weren't expecting.

✻ You might go from feeling *shamed* to feeling *enraged*. Shame and rage are very closely connected. Rage is a way to cover up shame so it doesn't show as much.

Just as the primary colors—red, yellow, and blue—can be mixed to make more colors, the nine types of feelings can blend to make more feelings. We call these combined feelings. Here are four you might experience.

Contempt

To feel *contemptuous* is to look down on other people. You think you're better than they are. You feel as if there's something wrong with them, and they don't deserve to be liked or respected.

Contempt is a combination of *anger* (page 33) and *dissmell* (pages 36–38). Sometimes contempt is a defense, a way to protect yourself against painful or uncomfortable feelings. For kids who feel left out or think they don't fit in, contempt is a way to prove it doesn't matter.

Times you might feel contemptuous are when:

- other kids seem slower than you or not as smart, and you feel superior to them

- you're lonely and you don't know how to make friends, so you decide you don't care or you don't need anyone

- other kids don't let you join their club, so you decide the club is stupid and not worth joining

- you're afraid to try something new but you don't want to show it, so you act above it all

- someone has insulted you and you want to get back at him or her

More names for contemptuous: scornful, disrespectful, stuck-up, smug, snooty, sarcastic
Opposites: modest, respectful, accepting, tolerant, admiring

Jealousy

To feel *jealous* is to feel bad inside because someone else has something you want. Or suddenly you have a rival for someone else's affections or attention. You feel less worthy or inferior—like there's something wrong with you. At the same time, you feel angry and resentful.

Jealousy is a combination of *shame* (page 35) and *anger* (page 33). Everyone feels jealous sometimes. It's a normal, natural feeling.

Times you might feel jealous are when:

- you get a new baby sister who's suddenly the center of attention— like *you* used to be

- your brother has a birthday party and gets lots of presents

- your best friend makes a new friend and no longer has much time for you

- your mom or dad spend more time with your brother or sister than they do with you

- kids at school won't let you join their clique or club

GET PERSONAL
Write about a time when you felt jealous. Tell what happened and what you did.

More names for jealous: envious, suspicious, resentful, possessive, bitter
Opposites: open-minded, tolerant, accepting, generous

Loneliness

To feel *lonely* is to feel like an outsider. You want to feel close to someone, or you want to belong to a group, but instead you feel shut out, ignored, and unwanted. It seems that no one understands you, wants to be with you, or cares about you.

Loneliness is a combination of *shame* (page 35) and *distress* (pages 31–32). We all need to feel like we belong somewhere, with someone. When we don't, we feel we're not good enough, and that makes us sad.

Times you might feel lonely are when:

- it seems that nobody wants to be your friend

- it seems that nobody likes you

- you've just switched schools, and you're having a hard time making friends

- you've just moved to a new neighborhood, town, or city where you don't know anyone

- everyone else in your family is busy, and no one has time for you

GET PERSONAL
Write about a time when you felt lonely. Tell what happened and what you did.

More names for lonely: isolated, alone, friendless, cut off
Opposites: connected, belonging, close, embraced

Down Mood

When your mood is up, you feel excited or joyful. When your mood is *down,* your head hangs low, your shoulders sag, and you might feel like crying.

Like loneliness, a down mood is a combination of *shame* (page 35) and *distress* (pages 31–32). You might feel down for one big reason, a lot of smaller reasons, or no specific reason at all—at least, not one you can name. You might feel down for a short time or a long time.

Some people use the word "depressed" to describe a down mood, but depression is different and more serious. If you ever experience a down mood that's *really* down and lasts for two weeks or longer, you might have depression. Talk with an adult you trust—a parent, teacher, or school counselor. Find someone who will listen and can help you feel better.

Times you might feel in a down mood are when:

- you keep failing a particular subject in school

- you keep getting picked on or teased by other kids

- you keep getting blamed for things at home

- a teacher at school often makes fun of you or ridicules you

GET PERSONAL
Write about a time when you were in a down mood. Tell what happened and what you did.

More names for a down mood: dejected, dispirited, downcast
Opposites: elated, upbeat, happy, joyful

Talk About Your Feelings

Talking about feelings should be a regular part of life. Unfortunately for many people, it isn't. They're uncomfortable talking about their own feelings. They're uncomfortable listening to other people talk about feelings. Maybe some of the adults in your life are like this.

Try to find someone you can talk to about your feelings. Start with your parents. Try a teacher, the school counselor, a youth group leader or religious leader. Maybe your brother or sister. You *will* find someone who speaks your language. You *will* find someone who listens and wants to understand.

Remember that feelings aren't wrong or right, bad or good. *Feelings just are.* All of your feelings are okay for you to have because they're *your* feelings. No one can take them away from you unless you let them. No one can make you change your feelings unless you let them. So don't! Claim your feelings as your own. They belong to you.

Name Your Future Dreams

Your future dreams are your personal goals. They give your life direction, purpose, and meaning. They guide your decisions and help you define the kind of person you are and want to be.

What happens if you don't have future dreams? You have no personal goals. You have nothing to give your life direction, purpose, and meaning. You have nothing to guide your decisions and help you define the kind of person you are and want to be. You're like a car without a steering wheel, or a ship without a rudder. Future dreams are important!

There are two kinds of future dreams: dreams for the *near future* and dreams for the *far future*. You need both kinds.

Examples of dreams for the near future are:

- to make friends at school with kids I respect
- to compliment at least one person every day
- to be healthy and fit
- to learn as much as I can about photography
- to read more and watch less TV
- to earn three more merit badges in Scouts
- to help other people in my neighborhood and community

GET PERSONAL

Write about your dreams for the near future. What are your personal goals for this week, next week, next month, or even a year from now? Make a list. Then think about ways to reach your personal goals. How can you make your dreams come true?

Examples of dreams for the far future are:

- to become a professional basketball player
- to become a dancer
- to become a scientist
- to someday have children of my own
- to get a job where I can work with animals
- to help make the world a better place

Look at what you've written about your near-future and
far-future dreams. Are they related? Do some of your near-
future dreams lead into your far-future dreams? If you want,
talk with an adult you trust about your future dreams. See if
he or she has any ideas that will help you reach your goals.

You may wonder where your future dreams come from.
You aren't born with them. You can't buy them at the mall.
In fact, they come from many different people and places.
Some of these are:

- your parents

- your teachers

- your religious leaders

- other people you look up
  to or admire—your role
  models

- your friends

- your peer group
  (people your age)

GANDHI

- the music you listen to

- what you read in books, magazines, and newspapers

- TV shows and movies

- your personal values—what you believe in and try to live by

- your imagination

Here's something else you should know about future dreams: Some may stay the same for many years or your whole life. Others will change as you grow and change. Get in the habit of listing your near-future and far-future dreams—once a month, once a year, or as often as you like. Keep track of your progress. In time, you'll have a map of your life showing where you've been and where you want to go. Naming your dreams adds to your personal power.

Name Your Needs

"Need" is a word we all use a lot. We talk about needing to see a new movie, or needing a faster Internet connection for our computer, or needing to get a haircut or a logo jacket.

But these aren't needs. These are *wants*. Needs and wants aren't the same.

There are seven basic needs that all people share:

1. the need for relationships with other people

2. the need for touching and holding

3. the need to belong and feel "one" with others

4. the need to be different and separate

5. the need to nurture (to care for and help other people)

6. the need to feel worthwhile, valued, and admired

7. the need for power in our relationships and our lives

Like feelings, needs aren't right or wrong, good or bad. *Needs just are.* The more you know about your needs, the more you can understand them and tell other people about them. And the more you can stick up for yourself.

The Need for Relationships with Other People

From the moment we're born, we need to care about other people. We need them to care about us. We need to feel *absolutely, positively sure* that we're important and wanted. We need to feel special in each of our relationships.

As you grow up and get older, some people may tell you, "It's not good to need or depend too much on other people. It's better to stand on your own two feet." We live in a culture that values independence. Our culture says that only weak people need other people.

In fact, it takes real strength to have relationships with people. Sometimes it's hard to be a friend, sister, brother, daughter, or son. Later in life, you may find out that sometimes it's hard to be a wife, husband, partner, or parent.

If you need other people, if you have relationships with other people, then you aren't weak. *You're strong.* Needing is a source of strength.

GET PERSONAL
Write about your most important relationships. Who are the people you care about most, and who care the most about you? Ask one of them to spend some time with you. (When you do this, you're asking to have your need met.) Later, write about what you did together and how you felt.

The Need for Touching and Holding

Babies, kids, teenagers, grown-ups, and grandparents—everyone needs to be touched and held sometimes.

Touching and holding are ways we show affection for one another. When your mom hugs you good-bye when you leave for school, she's saying, "I love you a lot."

Touching and holding are ways we comfort one another. When you fall off your bike and run to your dad and he holds you, he's saying, "I'm here to help you feel better."

Scientists know that babies need to be touched and held. When babies don't get enough touching and holding, they don't develop properly. They have physical and mental problems. Our need to be touched and held doesn't go away as we get older. We never outgrow it.

GET PERSONAL
Ask someone you trust for a hug. Write about what happens and how you feel.

Unfortunately, we live in a culture that confuses touching and holding with sex. That's why, as you get older, you may get mixed messages about touching and holding. Friends who touch each other are teased. Parents decide that their kids are too grown-up to be hugged and kissed. This is a problem with our culture; it isn't a problem with you. It's still okay to need touching and holding—now and for the rest of your life.

IMPORTANT: Of course, you should never let anyone touch you in ways that feel wrong to you. There's *good touch* and there's *bad touch*. Your parents and teachers have probably told you the difference. If they haven't, here are some basic tips to learn and remember: If someone (no matter who it is) tries to touch you in ways that make you feel funny, strange, uncomfortable, or afraid, trust your feelings. Say NO. Get away as fast as you can. And *tell an adult you trust.*

The Need to Belong and Feel "One" with Others

Thomas wants to grow up to be just like his dad. Rosa wants to grow up to be just like her mother. Josh looks up to his older brother. Kelly hopes that someday she'll be as smart as her teacher. And Will can't stop talking about his hero, a baseball player.

From an early age, we all have people we look up to and admire. And we want to be like them. We may copy the way they walk or dress and the things they say. This helps us feel like we're part of their lives, even part of them on the inside. We feel like we belong. We feel like we're "one" with them.

Another way we meet our need to feel "one" with others is by joining groups. Scouts, sports teams, computer club, and our faith community are all examples of groups we can join.

GET PERSONAL

Write about three people you look up to and admire. Who do you most want to be like? Why? Write about the groups or organizations you belong to. Tell what you like best about each one.

The Need to Be Different and Separate

We all need to feel different, separate, and unique. Each of us needs to believe that "there's no one else like me in the whole world."

We also need to be able to say to others, "I'm *not* you, I'm different from you." We may even need to say no to things they have taught us. This is how we define and discover who we really are and what we really believe.

The need to feel different and separate may seem like the opposite of the need to belong and feel "one" with others. In fact, it is. You'll go back-and-forth between these needs throughout your life. Sometimes you'll copy other people you admire. Sometimes you'll let your own talents, interests, and abilities lead the way.

GET PERSONAL

Write about three ways you're different from the people in your family. Write about three ways you're different from your friends. Be proud of your differences.

The Need to Nurture

AIESHA waits for her dad to take a nap. Then she quietly opens the door, goes outside, and starts washing the car.

Aiesha feels excited. Her dad doesn't know she's washing the car. It's a surprise! She thinks about what will happen when her dad wakes up. He'll come outside and see a clean, shiny car.

Aiesha knows that her dad will be happy. The whole time she works on the car, she feels good inside.

DAVID looks at the clock on the classroom wall. Only four more hours until the school roller-skating party! Everyone's going—kids, parents, teachers, even the principal.

"I'll be there," his teacher is saying. "But I'm not a good skater. I just hope nobody laughs at me!" She smiles to let the class know that she doesn't mind not being a good skater.

That night, at the rink, David sees his teacher. She's skating very slowly next to the rail.

David skates over to her. "Here," he says, "you can take my arm. I'll help you skate around the rink."

"Why, thank you, David!" his teacher exclaims. "This is really thoughtful of you."

David grins. He feels good inside.

We all need to nurture other people. We need to help them and show that we care about them.

Nurturing other people makes them feel good. It also makes *us* feel good inside.

GET PERSONAL

Write about three times when you helped other people. Tell how you felt and how they acted.

The Need to Feel Worthwhile, Valued, and Admired

Have you ever asked your mom, dad, or others to watch you do something—like play an instrument, dance, or shoot baskets? Do you remember the look in their eyes when they watched you?

We all need to feel worthwhile and valued. We need to feel recognized and openly admired.

At first, we count on other people to help us feel this way. In time, we learn to encourage and praise ourselves. Think of a baby who's just starting to walk. At first, she counts on her parents to help her stand up, lead her by the hand, and pick her up when she falls. In time, she learns to walk by herself.

When someone we care about says, "You're a good speller," we start to think, "I'm a good speller." When someone we care about says, "I like the way you talk to your little sister," we start to think, "I'm a kind person." As other people notice our talents and abilities, we feel more secure about them. We start to *know* that we're valuable and worthwhile, and that we *deserve* to be admired.

The Need for Power in Our Relationships and Our Lives

So far, we've been talking about personal power—being secure and confident inside yourself. But there's another kind of power we all need.

We need to feel that we have power in our relationships with other people. (This is not the same as having power *over* other people.) And we need to feel that we're in charge of our own lives.

Whenever you can make choices about things like what or when to eat, what to wear, bedtimes, or music lessons, you're exercising power. There are many things you don't have power over. But there are some things you *do* have power over.

Later, we'll tell you ways to get and use power in your relationships and your life. But first, there's something else you should know about your feelings, future dreams, and needs: how to claim them as your own.

Claim Your Feelings, Future Dreams, and Needs

MARIO can't find one of his winter gloves. He thinks he left it on the playground at recess. He knows there's a Lost-and-Found box in the school office. So he goes to the office after school and asks to see the Lost-and-Found box.

"I'm looking for my glove," he tells the school secretary. "It's blue with red stripes."

And there it is, sitting right on top of the box. "I found it!" he says. "This is my glove."

Mario *names* his glove. He doesn't say, "I'm looking for a mitten," or "I'm looking for a scarf." Then he *claims* his glove. He doesn't say, "This is my glove, but what's it doing here?" He doesn't say, "This is my glove, but it sure is ugly." He doesn't question or judge it. He simply accepts it. The glove belongs to him.

This is the way to claim your feelings, future dreams, and needs. Don't question or judge them. Simply *experience them, name them,* and *accept them.* They belong to you.

Why should you care about claiming your feelings, future dreams, and needs? Because naming them isn't enough to make them yours. What if Mario had said, "This is my glove," and then left it in the Lost-and-Found box? He would have known where to find his glove. But he wouldn't have been able to use it.

It's important to use *all* of your feelings, future dreams, and needs. Not just the ones that seem easy and safe. Not just the ones people say you should use.

* Maybe you don't like feeling shamed. You wish you could leave that feeling in a Lost-and-Found box forever.

* Or maybe one of your future dreams is turning out to be a pain. You really want to learn to play the trumpet. But learning means practicing, and practicing takes time.

* Or maybe you're having a problem with your need for touching and holding. It's embarrassing when your mom hugs you. Especially in front of your friends. Yet you like it when she hugs you, and you miss it when she doesn't…. Aarrgh! How confusing!

You may try to push away some feelings, future dreams, and needs, or lock them up inside yourself. This isn't a good idea, because they don't stay away or hidden. They can turn into problems later.

Many adults today have problems in their lives. Doctors and psychologists think it's because they denied or buried important feelings, future dreams, and needs when they were kids. When we do this, we lose track of who we are. We lose our *selves.*

Talk Things Over with Yourself

There's a simple way you can start claiming your feelings, future dreams, and needs. We call it "Talking Things Over with Yourself." Here's how it works:

1. **Ask yourself, "How am I feeling today?"** Then name a feeling you're having. Next, talk it over with yourself. Your talk might go something like this:

    Say: "I'm feeling sad today."

    Ask: "Why am I feeling sad? What's happened that I feel sad about?"

    Say: "I'm feeling sad because I had an argument with my dad last night."

    Ask: "What can I do about my sad feeling?"

    Say: "I can talk to my dad about the argument."

    Sometimes you can't change a feeling. But you can still talk it over with yourself. This is always better than pushing it away or locking it up inside yourself.

2. **Ask yourself, "What are my future dreams?"** Then name a dream for the near future or the far future. Next, talk it over with yourself. Your talk might go something like this:

    Say: "I want to work with animals someday."

    Ask: "What do I have to learn to make this dream happen?"

Say: "I can start by reading books about people who work with animals."

Ask: "What else can I do?"

Say: "I can talk to veterinarians and animal trainers."

3. **Ask yourself, "Is there anything I need right now?"** If the answer is yes, try to name your need. Then talk it over with yourself. Your talk might go something like this:

   Say: "I need to make friends at school. I feel left out and lonely sometimes."

   Ask: "How can I start making friends?"

   Say: "I can ask if anyone wants to shoot baskets with me at recess."

   Ask: "What if nobody says yes?"

   Say: "I can find another group of kids who are shooting baskets. I can ask if it's okay to play with them."

Sometimes you can't get what you need. But you can still talk it over with yourself. This is always better than pushing your need away or locking it up inside yourself.

TIPS FOR TALKING THINGS OVER WITH YOURSELF

* **Try to make this a habit. Set aside time to do it every day.**
* **Talk out loud to yourself, if you have a private place you can go to. If not, write down your questions and answers. Or just think them.**

When Feelings Are Too Strong to Handle: Great Escapes

Sometimes feelings are too strong to handle. Especially the ones that don't feel good. We get so distressed or fearful, shamed or angry that the feeling takes over.

At times like these, we may need to escape from our feeling for a while, until we're ready to deal with it. Here are four Great Escapes you can try.

Find something to laugh about

Read your favorite cartoon book. Watch a silly TV show. Ask somebody to tickle you or tell you a joke.

Maybe you can find something funny about what's bothering you. We know a man who does this. He used to drop and break things a lot. He felt angry at himself for being clumsy. He felt shamed because other people knew about him. He was often fearful that he would drop and break something else. One day, he found a way to laugh at this problem. Now, whenever he drops something, he says, "Uh-oh! Gravity strikes again!"

Focus on something else

Go swimming or bicycling. Shoot some baskets or lace up your skates. Take a walk and concentrate on the sights and sounds around you. Talk to yourself about everything you're seeing, hearing, smelling, and touching. This will take your mind off of your strong feeling.

Relax

Relaxing is another way to focus on something besides a strong feeling. There are many different ways to relax. Here's one you can try.

1. Find a quiet place where you can be alone for a while. Sit comfortably and close your eyes.

2. Picture yourself holding a huge bubble wand and a bottle of bubble soap. You dip your wand into the soap. You start blowing big rainbow bubbles. They float away, getting smaller and smaller, and finally disappear.

3. Put a worry inside each bubble. Watch your worry float away and disappear.

4. Do this for five or ten minutes. Stop when you feel ready.

Daydream

Daydreams are like owning your favorite movies on video. You can watch them as many times as you want, for free! You may already have your own special daydream for times when you need to "get away." Here are two more you can try.

"If I Could Have Whatever I Wanted..."

Sometimes we have strong feelings because we're pushing away or locking up another feeling, a future dream, or a need. This daydream can help you find out. Here are two examples.

1. "If I could have whatever I wanted...someone would adopt my brothers and sisters and take them away!" Maybe you're feeling jealous of them. Maybe you have the need to feel different and separate. What can you do to get your need met?

2. "If I could have whatever I wanted...my mom would rock me like she used to when I was a baby." Maybe you're feeling sad or fearful. Maybe you have the need for some touching and holding. What can you do to get your need met?

If you can't figure out what a daydream is telling you, talk it over with an adult you trust. Maybe he or she can help you explain your daydream.

Face Your Monster

Sometimes the best way to escape from something is to turn around and face it! This daydream helps you face the "monster" of your strong feeling.

1. Think about your feeling. Maybe it's fear or anger, shame or jealousy. Maybe it's loneliness or distress.

2. Now imagine what your feeling "looks" like.

   - Maybe fear looks like a tiny mouse. The mouse is shaking and its whiskers are quivering.

   - Maybe anger looks like a creature made of fire. Smoke is coming out of its ears and nose.

   - Maybe distress looks like a blue elephant. Its ears and trunk and tail are hanging down.

3. Now imagine yourself bringing your feeling a present. If your fear looks like a mouse, you could bring it a piece of cheese. If your anger looks like a fire creature, you could bring it an ice-cream cone. If your distress looks like a blue elephant, you could bring it some pink peanuts.

How to Deal with Strong Feelings

Great Escapes are great for times when feelings are too strong to handle. It's hard to think straight or know what to do when you're filled with a strong feeling. You need to get away from your feeling for a while. Later, when you're calm, you can think about your feeling, try to figure out what triggered it, and plan what to do when you have the feeling again.

But Great Escapes don't always work. Sometimes you return and the feeling is still there—maybe not as strong as it was, but strong enough to get in your way. And sometimes taking a Great Escape just isn't possible. You don't have time, or it's not the right time. You need to deal with the feeling *soon*, before it gets even stronger or you say or do something that might make things worse. Here are ideas to think about, talk about, and try.

Fear

1. Try to name your fear. Is it a strange noise? A threatening person? A storm? Ghosts? Monsters? Are you afraid that someone won't like you? That people will make fun of you? Be as specific as you can.

2. Decide if your fear is *realistic* or not. A realistic fear is something that could really happen. An unrealistic fear is something that isn't likely to happen.

3. If your fear is realistic, think about ways to face it, change it, or make it less frightening. How can you protect yourself? Who can help you?

4. If your fear is unrealistic, try to figure out why you're afraid. How would your life be different if you didn't worry about something that isn't likely to happen?

5. If you can't handle your fear on your own, *get help*. Talk with an adult you trust.

Distress

1. Try to name what's causing your distress. What are you sad about? Be as specific as you can.

2. Talk with someone about your distress—a parent, a brother or sister, a good friend who will listen.

3. Write about your distress or suffering. Describe your feeling. Tell why you feel that way. Keep writing until you're ready to stop. You might find that writing helps to relieve some or all of your distress.

4. Do something to cheer yourself up. Get together with a friend. Watch a favorite movie. Take a walk. Snuggle with your cat. Listen to music.

5. If you can't handle your distress on your own, *get help*. Talk with an adult you trust.

Anger

1. Try to name the reason why you're angry. Did someone insult you? Tease you? Treat you unfairly? Take out his or her anger on you? (That's not fair, but it happens, and when it does, you might feel angry back.) Be as specific as you can. Or maybe it was all a misunderstanding or an accident. Ask questions to find out. Maybe you don't have a reason to be angry.

2. If you *do* have a reason to be angry, try one or more of these ways to manage your anger.

    • If you feel like you're about to explode, walk away from the person or situation that's making you angry. If you can't walk away—for example, if a parent or teacher won't let you walk away—then take five deep breaths. Take five more. Or count to ten s-l-o-w-l-y. Do it again if you need to. Do whatever it takes to stop yourself from exploding. You can even ask for some time alone.

    • *Stop* and *think* before you speak or act. Will what you're about to say or do make things better or worse? If it's likely to make things worse, choose something else to say or do. Remember: You are responsible for your own behavior. What you say or do is up to you.

    • Tell yourself, "It's okay to feel angry. It's *not* okay to hurt someone back—even if he or she hurt me first."

    • Tense, then relax, every muscle in your body, from your head to your toes (or from your toes to your head).

- Change your anger habits. Instead of yelling back when someone yells at you, try this instead: Keep your voice low and calm. Say, "I hear what you're saying. You're saying that...." Instead of hitting back when someone hits you, walk away (if you can). Or stuff your hands deep in your pockets. Or clasp your hands behind your back.

- Let off steam in a positive way that won't hurt you or anyone else. Run around the block. Take a walk or a bike ride. Pound a pillow. Make paper balls and throw them against a wall. Shoot hoops. Jump up and down.

- Write a letter to the person you're angry at, as if you're speaking to him or her. But don't actually *send* the letter or give it to the person. Keep it to yourself. Writing the letter is just for you.

- Think peaceful thoughts. Imagine that you're on a beach, watching the waves roll in. Or lying on your back in a field, finding shapes in the clouds overhead. Or sitting on a block of ice, cooling down your hot, angry feelings.

3. Write about your anger. Describe the people and things that make you angry. Describe what you do when you're angry. Make a list of things you'd rather do instead. Set goals for yourself and write them down. Keep track of your progress.

4. If you can't manage your anger on your own, *get help.* Talk with your parents, teachers, school counselor, or other adults you trust. If anger is a big problem for you and other kids you know, you might ask your school counselor to start an anger management group at your school.

Shame

1. Try to name the source of your shame. Has someone said or done something to trigger your shame? Or does your shame come from inside?

2. Try to name the kind of shame you're feeling. Shame comes in different forms. You might feel worthless, powerless, embarrassed, discouraged, shy, guilty, self-conscious, or inferior.

3. Put words to your shame. Give it a voice. Tell someone you trust how you feel.

4. Be aware that shame can lead to anger—at yourself, at other people, at the world. Learn and practice ways to manage your anger.

5. Build your personal power and positive self-esteem. Be responsible for your behavior and your feelings. Name and claim your feelings, future dreams, and needs. This book is full of ideas that can help you.  When you feel secure and confident inside yourself, and when your self-esteem is healthy and strong, it's harder for other people to trigger your shame—and you feel stronger inside.

6. If you can't cope with shame on your own, *get help*. Talk with an adult you trust.

Jealousy

1. Try to name the reason for your jealousy. Did someone get something you wanted? Do you feel you're not getting enough attention? Does your best friend have a new friend? Be as specific as you can.

2. Be aware that jealousy can lead to anger—at yourself, at other people, at the world. Learn and practice ways to manage your anger.

3. Write about your jealousy. How does it make you feel? Does it get in the way of your friendships? Does jealousy cause you to say and do things you don't really mean—things that hurt you and other people? Would you like to stop being jealous?

4. Make a list of all the good things in your life. List the people you care about. The people who care about you. Your favorite possessions. What else makes you feel glad and grateful? Now list the things that make you feel jealous. You might find that your good things list is longer than your jealous list. This helps put things in perspective.

5. If you can't handle your jealousy—if it keeps you from enjoying life—*get help*. Talk with an adult you trust.

Loneliness

1. If you feel lonely, it's probably for one of two reasons. Either you spend too much time alone, or you spend too much time with the wrong people. Decide which reason is true for you.

2. If you spend too much time alone, do something about it. Make friends! Here are five tips to try:

   • Reach out. Don't wait for others to make the first move. If there's someone you'd like to know, say hi. Smile. Start a conversation. Find things you have in common. Spend time together.

   • Get involved. Join a group, troop, club, or team. Take a special class inside or outside of school that interests you.

   • Volunteer. Look for opportunities at school, in your neighborhood, in your community, in your place of worship.

   • Show other people that you're interested in them. Don't just talk about yourself. Ask questions about them. Be a good listener.

   • Be kind and respectful, tolerant and accepting. Treat other people the way you want them to treat you.

3. If you feel lonely when you're with your friends, maybe they aren't really your friends. Maybe they don't treat you very well. Maybe you don't have much in common. Maybe they're not a good influence on you, or they try to get you to do things you don't want to do. Break away and find new friends. You might feel more lonely for a while, but it won't last forever.

4. If you need help making friends or finding the right friends, talk with an adult you trust. Or talk with people your own age you respect and admire. Ask their advice.

Down Mood

1. Try to name the reason (or reasons) for your down mood. Be as specific as you can.

2. Write about your down mood. Let your feelings out.

3. Talk about your down mood with an adult you trust. Talk with friends who will listen and be supportive.

4. Tell yourself that everyone feels sad or blue sometimes. Gloomy feelings are part of life, and they usually pass.

5. Do something to cheer yourself up. Watch a funny video. Listen to a comedy tape or CD. Read a joke book. Spend time with someone who makes you laugh.

6. Get some exercise. Exercise releases chemicals in your brain called endorphins. Endorphins give you a natural high.

7. Remember that a down mood is different from depression. If your down mood lasts for two weeks or longer, talk with an adult you trust.

IMPORTANT: If you ever feel so down, sad, hopeless, or powerless that you think about hurting yourself, *get help right away.* Talk with an adult you trust. Or look in your Yellow Pages under "Crisis Hotline" or "Suicide Hotline" and pick up the phone. Don't wait!

GET AND USE POWER IN YOUR RELATIONSHIPS AND YOUR LIFE

CELIA can't wait to grow up. Maybe then she'll finally have some power over her own life.

Right now, it seems like everybody else gets to order her around. If she doesn't want to do something, she has to do it anyway or face the consequences. She hates that word—*consequences*. She hears it a thousand times a day.

Her mom orders her to make her bed. If she doesn't do it, the consequences are she's grounded until she does. Her dad orders her to walk the dog. If she doesn't do it, the consequences are no playing outside with her friends. Her teacher orders her to write a report. If she doesn't do it, first she gets an F on the assignment, and then she gets in trouble at home.

Plus there are other people who get to tell her what to do. The baby-sitter. Her big brother. Her Sunday-school teacher. Her gymnastics coach. Her piano teacher. Even her neighbor, Mrs. Marx. Last week, Mrs. Marx told her to stop bouncing her ball outside the apartment.

Celia wishes there could be *just one day* when she got to give the orders. She would make everybody sorry!

It's tough being a kid, and that's the truth. Anybody who tells you "this is the best time of your life" doesn't remember what it was like to be a kid!

What's so great about it, anyway? You're short. You can't drive. You have to go to school. You have to ask permission to go to the bathroom. Other people tell you to clean your room or wash your ears. You have to live where they say, wear what they say, eat what they say, even say what they say sometimes. It's the pits!

In fact, you have more power than you think. And you can use this power to stick up for yourself.

Two Kinds of Power

There are two kinds of power you should know about: *role power* and *personal power*.

Role power is built in to certain roles or jobs. Parents have role power over their kids. They get to make rules, give privileges, take privileges away, and more *just because they're parents.*

Teachers have role power over their students. They get to give assignments and tests, raise or lower grades, keep kids after school, send them to the principal's office or detention, and more *just because they're teachers.*

Many other people have role power. Including baby-sitters, Scout leaders, principals, and coaches. Police officers, lawmakers, judges, and presidents.

You might even have some role power yourself. If you're the leader of a club, head of the student council, or first chair in the school orchestra, then you have role power. You get to make decisions other people don't, *just because of your role.*

Role power and personal power are NOT the same. Here are some ways they're different:

* Role power is something you have just because you're in a certain role. Personal power is something you get because you want it and you work for it.

✴ Role power depends on having someone else to be powerful over. (A president without people to govern doesn't have much role power.) Personal power depends only on you.

✴ Role power is something you might have to wait for. You might never have very much role power. Personal power is something you can have *right now,* if you want it. And you can have as much as you want.

✴ Only some people can have role power. Anyone can have personal power. *You* can have personal power. *Even if many people have role power over you.*

It's important to understand these differences. Some people spend their whole lives fighting back against other people with role power. And some people think that role power is the only kind of power worth having. This causes problems in their lives.

Go back to page 72 and read Celia's story again. Can you see why Celia is having problems? She's angry with everyone who has role power in her life. She wishes she could get back at them. What a waste of energy!

What can Celia do instead? She can accept that some people have role power over her. She can work on building her personal power. Then she won't care so much that some people have role power over her. She'll feel secure and confident inside herself.

If you're always fighting back against people who have role power over you, is it doing any good? Probably not. It might even be getting you in trouble.

Here's an idea: Stop fighting back. Accept that some people have role power over you. Use your energy to build personal power. This is a way to stick up for yourself.

IMPORTANT: This doesn't mean you should *always* agree with people who have role power over you. Or that you should do *everything* they say. If an adult tries to get you to do something you don't feel right about, get help! Go to another adult you trust and can talk to. Tell that person what happened. Keep trying until you find someone who can help you.

Power in Your Relationships

EVAN and Dean live in the same neighborhood. Evan is in fourth grade, and Dean is in sixth grade. One day, Evan is riding his skateboard on the sidewalk when Dean walks by.

"Cool board," Dean says.

Evan is surprised that a big kid is talking to him, but he says, "Thanks. I got it for my birthday."

"I have a board, too," Dean says. "I can show you some tricks, if you want."

"Okay," Evan answers.

Dean gets his skateboard. For the next hour, the two boys skateboard together. Evan has a lot of fun. He likes Dean. And he wants Dean to like him, too.

When we care what someone else thinks of us, we give that person power over us. We act in ways we believe that person will like. We look up to that person and may start copying him or her.

Evan cares what Dean thinks of him. That's okay—as long as Dean treats Evan with respect. There are things Evan can learn from Dean. He can become a better skateboarder. But what if Dean doesn't treat Evan with respect? Maybe he makes fun of Evan or tries to teach him tricks that are too hard for him, even dangerous. That's *not* okay.

All through your life, you'll meet people whose opinions matter to you. You'll want them to like you, and you'll give them power over you. How will you know if they're treating you with respect? Pay attention to your feelings. If being with them and learning from them feels good and right inside, then do it. If it feels bad and wrong inside, or if it feels uncomfortable or funny, then *don't* do it.

You'll also meet people who care about what *you* think of *them.* This will make you feel powerful. How will you know if you're treating them with respect? Pay attention to your feelings. You'll know when you're acting in ways that are good for them—and when you're not.

Power and Choice

BEN is reading a book when his mom comes home from work.

"Have you finished your chores?" his mom wants to know.

"Not yet," Ben answers. "I got interested in this book. It's a great story about these two guys who decide to climb a mountain, and—"

"Put the book down RIGHT NOW," his mom interrupts. "Do your chores RIGHT NOW or you'll be grounded for a week!"

SAMANTHA is watching TV when her mom comes home from work.

"Have you finished your chores?" her mom wants to know.

"Not yet," Samantha answers. "I wanted to watch this program first."

"Samantha, we have a problem," her mom says. "You're supposed to do your chores when you come home from school."

"But this is my favorite program, and it's on right now!" Samantha exclaims.

"I understand that," her mom replies. "So let's see if we can find a solution to our problem."

Her mom thinks for a few moments. Then she says, "Maybe you can do your chores before you leave for school in the morning. Then you can watch your program when you come home. Or you can use the VCR to record your program while you do your chores. Then you can watch it later in the evening. Which do you choose?"

"I don't want to do my chores in the morning," Samantha says. "I guess I'll record the program and watch it later."

Her mom smiles. "Let's try that for a few days and see how it works."

Both Ben and Samantha have chores to do after school. In this way, they're the same. But Ben feels powerless while Samantha feels powerful. Why? Because Ben's mom gave him an order, and Samantha's mom gave her a choice.

Whenever we're given a choice, we feel powerful. Many parents and other people with role power know this. They try to give kids choices. Even if these are little choices, like "Which do you want first, the good-tasting medicine or the bad-tasting medicine?" The child can't choose whether to take the bad-tasting medicine. But he or she can choose *when* to take it. This helps the child feel powerful instead of powerless.

If you feel powerless at home, try talking with your parents. Tell them how you feel. Ask if they can give you choices about some things. This is a way to stick up for yourself.

Then, when you make a choice, *follow through.* Do what you say you'll do. For example, what if Samantha watches her program and doesn't do her chores? Her mom might take away her choice.

What if your parents won't give you choices? Even then, you don't have to be powerless. *You can give yourself choices.* Here are two you can think about:

✱ You can choose to accept things the way they are. If your parents don't want to change, you can't make them.

✱ You can choose to do a Great Escape. This will help if you're feeling frustrated, angry, sad, or shamed. You'll find some Great Escapes on pages 61–64.

Equal Power

NICK and Kareem live in the same apartment building. They often hang out together. They get along pretty well…as long as Nick does what Kareem wants. If he doesn't, Kareem threatens to go home. When this happens, Nick feels powerless. He doesn't want Kareem to go home, so he gives in.

Kareem has all the power in this relationship. He uses it to get his way. But there's something Nick can do to stick up for himself. The next time Kareem threatens to go home, Nick can smile and say, "Okay, see you later!"

This will surprise Kareem. Maybe he'll leave anyway. But maybe he'll stay. Nick will have to wait and find out.

By not giving in to Kareem, Nick will take back some of the power Kareem had all to himself. Now the two boys will have *equal* power.

ALIX and Kayla are friends. They enjoy playing together. But sometimes Kayla promises she'll come to Alix's house, and then she doesn't come. So Alix waits and waits.

Finally, Alix calls Kayla on the phone. Then Kayla says something like, "I'm sorry, I forgot." Or "I decided to stay home." Or "Hannah came over, and I'm playing with her instead."

When this happens, Alix feels powerless. She keeps expecting Kayla to keep her promises. She feels hurt, shamed, and angry when Kayla breaks her promises.

Kayla has all the power in this relationship. Alix can't change Kayla's behavior, but she can stick up for herself. Here are some things she can try:

- Alix can make new friends. Then she won't depend on Kayla so much.

- Alix can go to Kayla's house instead of calling her on the phone. Maybe Kayla will want to play with her. But maybe she won't. Alix will have to wait and see.

- Alix can try talking with Kayla about her behavior. She might tell Kayla how she feels when Kayla is disrespectful to her. Maybe Kayla doesn't know how her behavior affects her friend.

- Alix can stop expecting Kayla to follow through on her promises. We should be able to expect our friends to keep their word. But Kayla has broken a lot of promises in the past, so this isn't a realistic expectation for Alix to have.

Either way, Alix can take back some of the power Kayla had all to herself. Now the two girls will have *equal* power.

Tips to Try If You're Shy

Maybe you're thinking, "I'll never have equal power—or any power. I'm too shy!"

Guess what? Almost everyone feels shy at times. Shyness is shame in the presence of strangers. Surveys show that more than 90 percent of Americans say they've been shy at some point during their lives. Nearly half say they're still shy.

If you're shy, it might be hard for you to stick up for yourself. You might have trouble talking about your feelings, asking for what you need, and getting and using power in your relationships. You might have trouble forming relationships. Maybe your palms sweat and your heart races at the thought of saying hi to someone or starting a conversation.

If you want, you can try to be less shy. Here's how:

- Talk with adults you know and trust. Explain that you sometimes feel shy. Ask for help and ideas. Ask them to share stories about times when they felt shy.

- Start each day with a single goal. For example, "Today I'll say hi to at least one person in the hall." Or "Today, if James teases me, I'll tell him to stop."

- Make a mental list of three topics you feel comfortable talking about. Pick one and try starting a conversation with someone you'd like to know better.

- Make yourself do something you normally wouldn't do. Join a club. Invite someone over to your house. Offer to read aloud to younger kids at your school.

- Instead of saying no to invitations, say yes. The more time you spend with other people, the easier it gets.

- Make a new friend. The more friends you have, the less shy you'll feel.

- Build your positive self-esteem. Find ideas starting on page 91.

- Most of all, always respect yourself—even when you're feeling shy.

How to Deal with Bullies

If you've ever been bullied, you know how bad it feels. Bullying robs you of your personal power. It can leave you feeling helpless, inferior, shamed, afraid—and very angry.

Whether you're bullied once a month, once a week, or ten times a day, you don't have to take it anymore. Before you learn how to deal with bullies, here are five facts you should know:

1. If you're being bullied, it's not your fault. No one ever deserves to be bullied.

2. If you're being bullied, you're not alone. Bullying affects about five *million* elementary and junior high students in the United States, and millions more around the world.

3. Bullying is more than just teasing. Sometimes teasing can be fun, but bullying *always* hurts. Don't believe anyone who tells you that "bullying isn't a big deal" (it is) or "people who complain about bullies are babies" (they aren't) or "bullying is a normal part of growing up" (it's not). Bullying is a *big* problem.

4. There are three types of bullying:

- physical (hitting, pushing, kicking, punching, beating people up, etc.)

- verbal (name-calling, insults, racist or sexist comments, put-downs, etc.)

- emotional (ignoring, excluding, threatening, humiliating, rejecting, etc.)

5. If you're being bullied, you can do something about it. You can stick up for yourself in ways that work. And you can get help.

Here's what *not* to do and why:

- Don't cry, if you can avoid it. Bullies love having power over people. When you cry, you give them what they want.

- Don't try to get even. Bullies hate this. It makes them madder and meaner.

- Don't fight back physically. Bullies usually pick on people who are smaller and weaker than they are. You could get hurt.

- Don't make threats. Bullies respond to threats with more bullying.

- Don't ignore the bullying. Bullies want a reaction from the people they're picking on. If you ignore them, they'll try harder.

- Don't stay home from school. Bullies who can scare people away from school feel really powerful. Plus skipping school keeps you from learning.

Here's what you *can* do:

- Tell a friend—someone who will listen to you, support you, and stick up for you. Tell your parents, too.

- Tell a teacher. Especially if the bullying happens at school. Bullies are sneaky—they do most of their bullying where adults can't see or hear it. So your teacher might not know about the bullying unless you tell.

- When someone bullies you, stand up straight, look the bully in the eye, and say in a firm, confident voice, "Leave me alone!" Or "Stop it! I don't like that!" Bullies don't expect their victims to stick up for themselves. This might be enough to make them stop.

- Stay calm and walk away. Walk toward a crowded place or a group of your friends. Bullies usually don't pick on people in groups. They don't like being outnumbered.

Most schools today take bullying seriously. It's possible that your school or district is using a bully prevention program. Ask your teacher about this. Say that you want to learn more about how to stick up for yourself with bullies.

Power in Your Life

Even though you're "just a kid," you're a powerful person!
Think of the things you can do:

* **You can be responsible for your behavior and your feelings.** Nobody can make you do things you know you shouldn't do. Nobody can make you feel mad or sad, fearful or shamed.

* **You can make choices about your behavior and your feelings.** You can decide to be the kind of person other people can count on. You can choose to feel good about yourself. You can learn to make wise choices and have realistic expectations.

CHOICE = POWER

* **You can name and claim your feelings.** You can tell other people how you feel. You can stick up for your feelings.

* **You can name and claim your future dreams.** You can decide what is important to you. You can stick up for your future dreams and work to make them come true.

* **You can name and claim your needs.** You can understand your needs. You can stick up for your needs and work to get them met.

* **You can take a Great Escape when your feelings get too strong to handle.** You can "step outside" your feelings and let them go, or calm down and deal with your feelings later.

* **You can get power in your relationships with
  other people.** You can make choices so you won't
  feel powerless. You can try to get equal power in
  some of your relationships.

All of these things add up to *personal power*. You can use
your personal power in all parts of your life. You can feel
secure and confident inside no matter where you are, who
you're with, or what you're doing. With personal power,
you really are in charge of your own life!

HOW TO LIVE HAPPILY EVER AFTER

Here's how it happens in fairy tales: A poor, powerless man
turns out to be a king, marries a princess, and they live happily ever after. Or a poor, powerless woman gets noticed by
a prince, they marry, and they live happily ever after.

It would be great if things worked out that way in real
life. But they don't. In fact, there's no such thing as "living
happily ever after."

You are responsible for your own happiness. Other people
can care about your happiness, but no one else can *make* you
happy. Only you can choose how you face life and how you
feel about yourself. And even you can't make yourself
happy all of the time.

We live in a culture that tells us to *expect* happiness. If we
aren't happy, there must be something wrong with us. But
this isn't a realistic expectation. Real life is full of surprises.
You'll have good days and bad days. You'll be happy sometimes and sad sometimes.

What you can do is learn to *collect and store happiness* so you always have a supply.

Keep a Happiness List

Some people store good feelings inside themselves and let go of bad ones. Other people do just the opposite. Which kind are you? Here's a way to find out:

 Write down five things that happened yesterday. These should be the first five things that come to your mind.

When you finish writing, read your list. Did you remember five good things, five bad things, or some of each?

You can choose what things to remember and make a part of you. You can learn to remember good feelings and let go of bad ones. Here's how:

 Write down five things that happened today— things you feel good about that put a smile on your face.

These don't have to be Big Things. If you wait to get straight A's or win a million dollars, you may never write a word. Instead, think about the small things you usually don't notice that make you feel good inside.

- Did the sun shine today?

- Did your teacher give you a compliment?

- Did you get to pet a puppy... or a kitten, or a hamster?

- Were your new shoes comfy?

- Did your mom or dad give you a hug?

- Did a friend let you borrow a favorite toy?

- Did you smile at someone you like a lot...
  and did he or she smile back at you?

- Did a funny joke make you laugh?

- Did you eat your favorite food for lunch?

- Did you get a letter or email from a friend?

- Did you learn something new and exciting
  in school?

- Did you spend time with people you care about?

- Did you find an extra dollar in the bottom of your
  backpack?

All of these things and more could go on your Happiness
List.

DO THIS EVERY DAY.
WEEKDAYS AND WEEKENDS.
SCHOOL DAYS AND HOLIDAYS.
BE HAPPY 5 TIMES
EVERY DAY.

You can do it before you go to bed at night. Or keep a
notebook in your pocket and do it throughout the day.

It won't always be easy to remember good things. There will be days when you really have to work at it. But don't give up. You can do it...and it's worth it.

Why is it so important to make a Happiness List every day? There are five reasons (and maybe more):

1. It boosts your *personal power.*

2. It teaches you that *you are responsible* for your own happiness.

3. It teaches you that *you can choose* how to experience your life.

4. It teaches you to look for things that *create* happiness.

5. It teaches you how to *collect and store* good feelings.

Think of this as a "happiness savings account." The next time you feel sad or depressed, angry or fearful, you can go to your savings account, take out a good feeling, and actually *feel* it all over again. This will turn your attention away from your bad feeling.

From now on, whenever something happens that puts a smile on your face:

1. **STOP** everything and notice what's making you happy, then

2. **FEEL** the happy feeling, then

3. **STORE** it inside of you, then

4. **WRITE** it down as soon as you can.

TIPS FOR MAKING THE MOST OF YOUR HAPPINESS LIST

* Do it with a parent or your whole family. This is a great habit for everyone to get into.

* Keep your Happiness List in a special note-book or folder. Decorate your notebook or folder any way you choose.

* Every so often, read through your Happiness List and enjoy your good feelings again.

* Every so often, look through your Happiness List and pick something to experience again. If you wrote, "I took a walk with my mom," invite her to take another walk with you. If you wrote, "I saw the sunset," watch the sun-set again.

HOW TO BUILD POSITIVE SELF—ESTEEM

It's the first day of school. You've found your classroom, said hi to your friends, and taken a seat. You notice that the teacher is a new face—someone you haven't seen before. He stands in front of his desk and smiles at everyone who comes into the room. The bell rings and you wait to see what will happen next.

The teacher walks to the board and writes his name in big letters: "MR. CARL MORSE." Then he writes a list of phrases after his name, like this:

> 1. TEACHER FOR 10 YEARS
>
> 2. LOVING HUSBAND AND DAD—TWO GREAT KIDS
>
> 3. COACH OF NEIGHBORHOOD SOFTBALL TEAM
>
> 4. VOLUNTEER AT BIG BROTHERS/BIG SISTERS
>
> 5. SAXOPHONE PLAYER IN A JAZZ BAND

He turns to the class and says, "Now you know my name and something about me. These are five things I'm proud of. I want to start the year by learning something about each of you. Please take out a piece of paper, write your name at the top, then write five good things about yourself—things you're proud of."

Do you start writing...or stare at the paper? Can you think of five good things about yourself? Five things that make you proud to be you?

Do you have enough positive self-esteem?

To stick up for yourself, you need personal power *and* positive self-esteem. *You need to believe that you're worth sticking up for.*

How would you rate your self-esteem? Here's a quick way to find out.

SELF—ESTEEM QUIZ

For each question, pick the response that's closest to the way you talk to yourself, think about yourself, or feel about yourself.

1. **When you get up in the morning and look at yourself in the mirror, what do you say?**

    (a)   "I look great this morning! And I'm going to have a great day."

    (b)   "Oh, no, not me again! I'm so ugly! Why did I bother to get out of bed?"

2. **When you fail at something or make a mistake, what do you tell yourself?**

    (a)   "Everyone has the right to fail or make mistakes every day. Including me."

    (b)   "I blew it again! I can't do anything right! I should have known better."

3. **When you achieve something, what do you say to yourself?**

   (a) "I'm proud of myself."

   (b) "I could have done even better if I had tried harder. It wasn't good enough."

4. **You've just talked with someone who has role power over you. (Like a parent, a teacher, or a coach.) What do you tell yourself?**

   (a) "I handled that pretty well."

   (b) "I can't believe I acted so stupid! I always say dumb things."

5. **You've just left the first meeting of a new club you joined. What do you say to yourself?**

   (a) "That was fun. I met some people I liked. They even laughed at the joke I told."

   (b) "I talked too much, and nobody liked me. Everyone hated my joke."

6. **You've just left a friend's house after playing together. What do you tell yourself?**

   (a) "That was fun. We really like each other!"

   (b) "My friend was just pretending to like me. I probably won't get invited back ever again."

7. **When someone gives you a compliment, what do you say to yourself?**

   (a)   "That's nice, and it makes me feel good. Besides, I deserve it!"

   (b)   "Nobody gives you a compliment unless they want something back. Besides, I don't deserve it."

8. **When someone you care about lets you down, what do you tell yourself?**

   (a)   "My feelings are hurt, but I'll get over it. Later, I can try to find out what happened."

   (b)   "This proves that person doesn't care about me."

9. **When you let down someone you care about, what do you say to yourself?**

   (a)   "It isn't nice, and it isn't fun, but sometimes people let each other down. I'll admit what I did, say I'm sorry, hope the person will forgive me, and get on with my life."

   (b)   "How could I do such a terrible thing? I'm so ashamed. No wonder nobody likes me."

10. **When you feel needy or unsure of yourself, what do you tell yourself?**

   (a)   "Everyone feels this way sometimes. I'll ask my dad for a hug or curl up with my Teddy bear, and I'll feel better soon."

   (b)   "Why can't I grow up and stop being a baby? What's wrong with me?"

Scoring: Give yourself 10 points for every (a) answer and 5 points for every (b) answer. Then use the key below to find your Self-Esteem Rating.

POINTS	RATING
90–100	Your self-esteem is HIGH and POSITIVE.
75–90	Your self-esteem is OKAY. Read on to learn ways to strengthen it.
60–75	Your self-esteem is SHAKY. But now you know it, and you can choose to change it.
50–60	Your self-esteem is LOW. Luckily, there are lots of things you can do to raise it…starting today.

WHAT SELF—ESTEEM REALLY MEANS

Before you learn ways to raise your self-esteem, it's important to know what self-esteem really means.

You might have heard people talk about self-esteem as if it's a bad thing. They think self-esteem means bragging, being stuck-up, and believing you're better than everyone else.

They're mistaken.

Self-esteem means being proud of yourself and feeling that pride on the inside. Not because you've told yourself, "I'm special and wonderful." Not because other people have said, "You're special and wonderful." Words don't create pride. Actions create pride. *Self-esteem means being proud of yourself because you've done things you're proud of.*

Maybe you've set personal goals and reached them. Maybe you've achieved or accomplished good things. Maybe you've handled tough situations well. Maybe you've treated other people with kindness and respect. Or maybe you've lived your life so far in a way that makes you proud—staying true to your values and beliefs, and true to yourself.

Self-esteem isn't about feeling superior to other people. It has nothing to do with anyone else. It's just about *you.*

Here are a few more myths and facts about self-esteem:

MYTH	FACT
Self-esteem comes from the outside—from people who praise you and compliment you.	**Self-esteem comes from inside—from knowing yourself and the kind of person you are.**
Self-esteem can be given to you and taken away.	**Self-esteem is learned and earned.**
Self-esteem is the cause of success.	**Self-esteem is the result of being proud of yourself for your actions, and also for the person you are.**

10 REASONS WHY YOU NEED SELF—ESTEEM

When you have self-esteem:

1. You're more likely to take positive risks. You know you might fail, but you also know you might succeed.

2. You're less likely to take negative risks. You respect yourself too much to put yourself in danger.

3. You're more likely to resist negative peer pressure.

4. You're less likely to go along with the crowd just to fit in.

5. You're strong. You can cope with the changes and challenges of life.

6. You're resilient. You can bounce back when life pounds you down with problems, disappointments, or failures.

7. You set goals for yourself and strive to reach them.

8. You feel free to explore your creativity and make the most of your talents, skills, and abilities.

9. You can let yourself be happy because you know you're worth it.

10. You have a positive attitude toward life.

WAYS TO BUILD YOUR SELF—ESTEEM

Keep an I—Did—It List

You are responsible for your own self-esteem. Other people can try to build it up (or break it down), but no one else can *make* you feel more or less proud of yourself.

You can learn to *collect and store pride* so you always have a supply. The I-Did-It List is like the Happiness List described on pages 87–90. But instead of writing down things that happened, you write down things you did or ways you acted.

Write down five things you did or ways you acted yesterday.

When you're done writing, read your list. Did you remember five good things? Or five not-so-good things? Or some of each?

You can choose what things to remember for your I-Did-It List. Pick things you feel proud of. Like:

- activities you took part in
- problems you solved
- decisions you made
- challenges you met
- successes you achieved
- goals you reached
- positive risks you took
- people you helped

 Write down five things you did or ways you acted today that made you feel proud of yourself.

At first, it might be hard to think of even one. Keep trying! These don't have to be Big Things. You don't have to win the Nobel Prize, climb Mount Everest, or end world hunger. You don't have to be a hero or a star.

You'll find that you do good things and act in positive ways when you're just being yourself. Your list might include things like this:

- I cleaned my room without being told.
- I got to school on time.
- I studied hard for the math quiz, and think I got 8 out of 10 answers right. (I'll find out for sure tomorrow.)
- I was nice to the new kid in school.

- I gave a speech in front of my class. I was scared, but I made it all the way through without freezing up!

- I tried out for the soccer team.

- When our gerbil escaped from its cage, I helped to find it.

- I set the table for dinner (and did a good job, too).

- When my little sister fell down and scraped her knee, I held her until she stopped crying. Then I washed off the scrape and put a Band-aid on it.

- My dad blamed me for breaking the window. I told him what really happened—it was an accident. I stayed calm the whole time, and offered to help him fix it.

DO THIS EVERY DAY.
WEEKDAYS AND WEEKENDS.
SCHOOL DAYS AND HOLIDAYS.
BE PROUD OF YOURSELF
5 TIMES EVERY DAY.

Why is it good to keep an I-Did-It List? (You might choose to call it your "Pride List.") It helps you to stick up for yourself *with yourself*. Sometimes you might forget that you're valuable and worthwhile. The I-Did-It List reminds you. It gives you proud feelings every day.

Think of your I-Did-It List as a "self-esteem savings account." The next time you feel your self-esteem falling, look at your list. Remember how it felt to do good things. This will boost your self-esteem, and you'll feel better about yourself again.

From now on, whenever something happens that makes you feel proud:

1. **STOP** everything and notice what's making you proud, then

2. **FEEL** the proud feeling, then

3. **STORE** it inside of you, then

4. **WRITE** it down as soon as you can.

TIPS FOR MAKING THE MOST OF YOUR I—DID—IT LIST

* Do it with a parent or your whole family. This is a great habit for everyone to get into.

* Keep your I-Did-It List in a special notebook or folder. Decorate your notebook or folder any way you choose.

* Every so often, read through your I-Did-It List and enjoy your accomplishments again.

* Every so often, look through your I-Did-It List and pick something to experience again. If you wrote, "I helped my dad mow the lawn," ask him if the lawn needs mowing and offer to help. If you wrote, "I made dinner for my family," start planning tonight's menu.

Use Positive Self—Talk

When you have a negative or critical thought about yourself, replace it with a positive thought. When your inner voices are mean to you, talk back! Instead of focusing on something you're frustrated or anxious about, think about something you're proud of.

CHANGE THIS...	INTO THIS...
"I can't do anything right."	**"I can build a great campfire."**
"Nobody wants to be my friend."	**"I can be a friend to someone."**
"I'm so stupid sometimes!"	**"I know a lot about animals. Especially dogs."**
"What if nobody likes my science fair project?"	**"I worked really hard on my science fair project, and I'm proud of it."**

It will take time before this feels natural. For some adults, it can take a year or more. We believe kids learn faster than adults, so maybe it won't take that long for you.

Spend Time with People Who Love You

Especially as you get older, your friends will become more interesting than your family. You'll want to spend more time with your friends, less time with your parents, brothers and sisters, grandparents, aunts and uncles, and other family members.

Relatives can be a pain, but they give you something other people can't: *Unconditional love and acceptance.* True, they also pick on you. But this makes their praise and compliments more precious.

Unconditional love and acceptance are powerful self-esteem builders. If a stranger came up to you and said, "You're the best, smartest, greatest kid in the world," you'd run the other way as fast as you could. If your grandma said it, you'd smile, give her a hug, and believe every word.

Do Good for Others

There are many ways you can help others and make a difference in the world. Look around you. Ask friends, neighbors, and family members for ideas. Talk with your parents, teachers, community leaders, and religious leaders.

What about doing a service project with your family? Joining or starting a service club at your school? Getting involved with a club, group, troop, or team that's active in community service? Boy Scouts of America, Girl Scouts of the U.S.A., Girls, Inc., Campfire, and 4-H all give kids opportunities to serve.

Your service doesn't have to be organized. You might spend an hour each week picking up trash in your neighborhood. Or reading to an elderly neighbor. Or watching little kids while their parents do chores. And don't forget to help out at home.

16 SURE SIGNS OF STRONG SELF-ESTEEM

Your self-esteem is strong when:

1. It doesn't depend on whether things always go right in your life.

2. You enjoy your successes because they make you feel proud inside, not because other people praise you.

3. You do good things for others without expecting anything in return.

4. You're not afraid to talk about your talents and abilities, but you don't exaggerate or brag.

5. You don't worry too much about failing or looking foolish.

6. You don't make excuses for your mistakes. You claim them and learn something useful from each one.

7. You're assertive—you say what you want and need—but not bossy.

8. You're mostly happy with yourself the way you are.

9. You don't need to put other people down to feel good about yourself.

10. You can do many things for yourself, but you ask for help when you need it.

11. You accept compliments, but you don't get a swelled head.

12. You listen to criticism, but you don't let it drag you down.

13. You don't get defensive when someone questions you.

14. You don't get angry when someone challenges you.

15. You care about achievement, but you don't push yourself too hard or try to be perfect.

16. You can laugh at yourself.

What to Do When Your Self—Esteem Starts to Fall

Throughout your life, your self-esteem will rise and fall. You'll feel better about yourself on some days and not so great on others. That's normal and natural. Two reasons why self-esteem falls are powerlessness and shame.

What can you do when you have that sinking feeling? When, for whatever reason, your self-esteem starts to fall?

It's not enough to think positive thoughts. You must take *positive action*. For ideas and inspiration, read your I-Did-It List. Then add to it by doing things that build your self-esteem.

SELF—ESTEEM DO'S AND DON'TS

DO expect to make mistakes. We believe that every human being has the right to make FOUR BIG MISTAKES every day. That includes you.

DON'T compare yourself to other people. This is a hard habit to break. We live in a culture that teaches us to compare. Parents compare their children. Teachers compare their students. Remember that you're one of a kind. There's nobody else in the world exactly like you.

DO give yourself permission to fail. Just because you fail at something doesn't mean *you* are a failure. Everybody fails sometimes. Nobody's perfect.

DON'T worry so much about what other people think of you. Most of us feel anxious about meeting new people. We wonder, "What will they think of me? Will they like me? Will they think I'm dumb? Will they think I'm boring?" Worrying makes us even more anxious. It also makes us feel powerless, self-conscious, and shamed.

You can choose to change your thinking. You can wonder, "What will I think of them? Will I like them? Will I think they're interesting?" Then you have equal power and no shame.

DO keep challenging yourself. Think of your self-esteem as a spiral moving up. When your self-esteem is strong, you face new challenges with confidence. When you succeed, your self-esteem grows. You can face more challenges with greater confidence. And on and on. Sometimes you'll fail, but you'll cope...because your self-esteem is strong.

DON'T set unreachable goals for yourself. If you try and fail over and over, rethink your goal. Pretend you're a high-jumper; lower the bar. Tomorrow is another day.

DO treat yourself like a worthwhile person. Give yourself plenty of praise—for the good things you do, the capable person you are, and the positive way you live your life.

DON'T blame yourself when things go wrong in your life. And don't accept any blame that others try to put on you, even adults. Blame is not the same as responsibility. Blame is negative. Responsibility is positive. Blame creates negative feelings—"I'm no good," "I was wrong," "I'm a bad person." Responsibility creates positive feelings—"I did this, and I can try to make it right," "I can do better next time." Remember that you're responsible only for *your* behavior and *your* feelings, not anyone else's. It's not "your fault" if your mom gets angry. It's not "your fault" if your softball team loses the game.

DO make Happiness Lists and I-Did-It Lists every day. They really will help you to collect and store good feelings and positive self-esteem.

SIX GOOD THINGS TO DO FOR YOURSELF

1. **Choose something to do just for fun.** Then do it whenever you can. Go swimming, go swinging, build models. Paint pictures, play basketball, draw cartoons. Write stories, be a clown, design your own Web site. And forget the old saying, "Anything worth doing is worth doing well." Don't try to be perfect. Don't aim to be an expert at everything. Keep some things just for fun.

2. **Give yourself a treat every day.** This can be almost anything, as long as it's just for you. Listen to your favorite music. Take a bubble bath. Play with your LEGOs. Learn a joke.

3. **Forgive yourself for something you did in the past.** We've all done things we wish we hadn't done. We've all hurt someone else's feelings. But we don't have to feel sad, guilty, or shamed forever.

   Pick something you did in the past. Remember it one last time. Think about everything that happened. What did you do? What did you say? Were other people involved? What did they do or say? What were the consequences? Did you get punished? Now close your eyes and say, "I'm sorry, and I forgive myself."

4. **Do at least one thing every day that's good for your body**. Get physical. Take a walk, ride your bike, go for a run, or do some sit-ups. You'll stay fit and healthy—and you'll feel better about yourself. Physical activity boosts self-esteem, promotes a positive body image, and helps you feel good about yourself.

5. **Do at least one thing every day that's good for your brain.** Solve a puzzle or do a brain-teaser. Read a book. Memorize part of a song, poem, or play. Listen to a concert on the radio. Visit a museum (for real or online). Learn something new.

6. **Find adults you can trust and talk to.** Being a kid is scary sometimes. Caring adults can help you face your fears. Being a kid is confusing sometimes. Caring adults can help answer your questions. Maybe not *all* of them, but at least some of them.

   Let your feelings guide you to the right people. Pick three or more you feel safe with. Pick those who care enough to listen and try to understand how you feel. This is one of the *best* things you can ever do for yourself.

YOU CAN STICK UP FOR YOURSELF

Do you remember Tyler, Ashley, and Jose? Tyler got hassled at school. Ashley's parents blamed her for everything. Jose's study hall teacher wasn't fair. If you want, you can read their stories again on pages 1–2.

Imagine that Tyler, Ashley, and Jose know the ideas you've been learning in this book. They know about personal power and positive self-esteem. They know how to stick up for themselves. Here's what happens.

TYLER

The next time kids hassle him, Tyler stands up straight, looks them in the eye, and says in a firm, confident voice, "Leave me alone! I don't like this, and I won't put up with it anymore." Then he calmly walks away.

Over the next few weeks, Tyler works hard to make friends. He starts hanging out with other kids in his class, and he joins an after-school club. Soon, he's not alone as much as he used to be—and he's not as easy to pick on and tease. Tyler feels better about himself and school.

ASHLEY

The next time Ashley's parents blame her for something she didn't do, she stands up straight, looks them in the eye, and says in a firm, confident voice, "Mom, Dad...can we talk about something important? If now isn't a good time, how about later today?"

Her parents agree on a time to talk, and Ashley comes prepared.

"I feel like I get blamed for everything," Ashley begins. "Even things that aren't my fault. I know I'm not perfect, but I do the best I can. Before you blame me for something, can we talk about what really happened? If it's my fault, I'll take responsibility and try to fix it. Or I'll take the consequences. Okay?"

That night, Ashley meets her friend in the chat room.

"Guess what?" she spells out on her keyboard. "I stuck up for myself with my parents. I asked them to stop blaming me for stuff, plus I said I'd be more responsible. Maybe things will get better around my house. I know I feel better!"

JOSE

Jose returns to school the next day and asks to speak privately to his study hall teacher.

He starts by saying, "I know I broke the rule about not talking. But could you listen to my side of the story?" Then he calmly explains about Matthew kicking him under the table. He asks if he can be seated somewhere else, away from Matthew. The teacher agrees to give it a try.

Then Jose asks, "If something like that ever happens again, what can I do so I don't break the rule?"

"You can raise your hand," the teacher suggests. "Then I'll come over and give you permission to talk."

"Thanks," Jose says. "I'll remember that."

When you have personal power, you feel secure and confident inside yourself. You can make choices and decisions. When you have positive self-esteem, you're proud of yourself and feel that pride on the inside.

Personal power and positive self-esteem are skills you can learn, like reading, writing, and arithmetic. You've learned the basics from reading this book. You know what you need to get and use personal power and build your self-esteem. So *you* can stick up for yourself—starting today.

INDEX

ABOUT THE AUTHORS

Gershen Kaufman was educated at Columbia University and received his Ph.D. in clinical psychology from the University of Rochester. Professor in the Counseling Center and Psychology Department at Michigan State University, he is the author of *Shame: The Power of Caring* (Rochester, Vermont: Schenkman Books, 1992) and *The Psychology of Shame: Theory and Treatment of Shame-Based Syndromes* (New York: Springer Publishing Co., 1996). He is the coauthor with Lev Raphael of *Dynamics of Power: Fighting Shame and Building Self-Esteem* (Rochester, Vermont: Schenkman Books, 1991) and *Coming Out of Shame* (New York: Doubleday, 1996).

Lev Raphael was educated at Fordham University and received his M.F.A. in Creative Writing from the University of Massachusetts at Amherst. He holds a Ph.D. in American Studies from Michigan State University, where he has taught as an assistant professor of American Thought and Language. With Gershen Kaufman, he codeveloped and cotaught the program, "Affect and Self-Esteem," on which *Dynamics of Power* and *Stick Up for Yourself!* are based. Book critic for National Public Radio's "The Todd Mundt Show" and "Mysteries" columnist for *The Detroit Free Press,* he is the author of three Nick Hoffman mysteries, most recently *The Death of a Constant Lover* (New York: Walker & Co., 1999).

Pamela Espeland has authored and coauthored many books for children and adults including *What Kids Need to Succeed, What Teens Need to Succeed, Making the Most of Today,* and *Making Every Day Count,* all for Free Spirit Publishing.

Other Great Books from Free Spirit

A Teacher's Guide to Stick Up for Yourself!
A 10-Part Course in Self-Esteem and Assertiveness for Kids
Revised and Updated Edition
by Gershen Kaufman, Ph.D., Lev Raphael, Ph.D., and Pamela Espeland
Reinforces and expands the messages of the student book with a step-by-step curriculum in ten easy-to-use sessions.
For teachers, grades 3–7.
$19.95; 128 pp.; softcover; 8½" x 11"

Psychology for Kids
40 Fun Tests That Help You Learn About Yourself
by Jonni Kincher
Based on sound psychological concepts, these fascinating tests promote self-discovery, self-awareness, and self-esteem and empower young people to make good choices.
For ages 10 & up.
$16.95; 152 pp.; softcover; illus.; 8½" x 11"

Making the Most of Today
Daily Readings for Young People on Self-Awareness, Creativity, & Self-Esteem
by Pamela Espeland and Rosemary Wallner
Quotes from famous figures guide you through a year of positive thinking, problem solving, and practical lifeskills, the keys to making the most of every day.
For ages 11 & up.
$9.95; 392 pp.; softcover; 4¼" x 6¼"

Making Every Day Count
Daily Readings for Young People on Solving Problems, Setting Goals, & Feeling Good About Yourself
by Pamela Espeland and Elizabeth Verdick
Each entry in this book of daily readings includes a thought-provoking quotation, a brief essay, and a positive "I"-statement that relates the entry to the reader's own life.
For ages 11 & up.
$9.95; 392 pp.; softcover; 4¼" x 6¼"

Worth the Risk
True Stories About Risk Takers Plus How You Can Be One, Too
by Arlene Erlbach
In an era when risk taking is most often associated with dangerous behavior or poor choices, this uplifting book points out the benefits of taking a chance. Includes 20 first-person stories about young risk takers plus step-by-step advice on how to take risks, set goals, and more.
For ages 10–15.
$12.95; 136 pp.; softcover; B&W photos; 6" x 9"

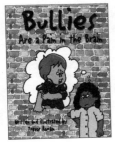

Bullies Are a Pain in the Brain
written and illustrated by Trevor Romain
Bullies are a pain in the brain—and every child needs to know what to do when confronted by one. This book combines humor with serious, practical suggestions for coping with bullies.
For ages 8–13.
$9.95; 112 pp.; softcover; illus.; 5⅛" x 7"

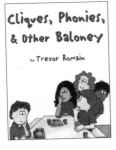

Cliques, Phonies, & Other Baloney
by Trevor Romain
Written for every kid who has ever felt excluded or trapped by a clique, this book blends humor with practical advice as it tackles a serious subject.
For ages 8–13.
$9.95; 136 pp.; softcover; illus.; 5⅛" x 7"

*To place an order or to request a free catalog of SELF–HELP FOR KIDS®
and SELF–HELP FOR TEENS® materials, please write, call, email, or
visit our Web site:*

Free Spirit Publishing Inc.
217 Fifth Avenue North • Suite 200 • Minneapolis, MN 55401-1299
toll-free 800.735.7323 • local 612.338.2068 • fax 612.337.5050
help4kids@freespirit.com • www.freespirit.com

Visit us on the Web!

www.freespirit.com

Stop by anytime to find our Parents' Choice Approved catalog with fast, easy, secure 24-hour online ordering; "Ask Our Authors," where visitors ask questions—and authors give answers—on topics important to children, teens, parents, teachers, and others who care about kids; links to other Web sites we know and recommend; fun stuff for everyone, including quick tips and strategies from our books; and much more! Plus our site is completely searchable so you can find what you need in a hurry. Stop in and let us know what you think!

Just point and click!

new! Get the first look at our books, catch the latest news from Free Spirit, and check out our site's newest features.

contact Do you have a question for us or for one of our authors? Send us an email. Whenever possible, you'll receive a response within 48 hours.

order! Order in confidence! Our secure server uses the most sophisticated online ordering technology available. And ordering online is just one of the ways to purchase our books: you can also order by phone, fax, or regular mail. No matter which method you choose, excellent service is our goal.

1.800.735.7323 • fax 612.337.5050 • help4kids@freespirit.com

REVISED AND UPDATED!

STICK
UP FOR
YOURSELF!

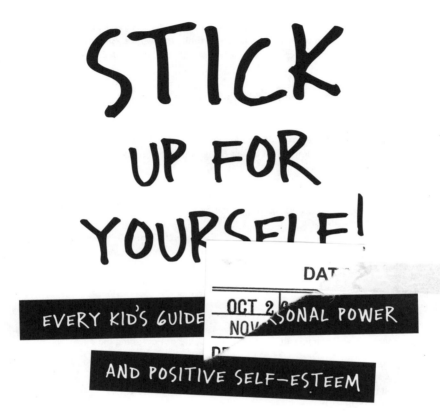

EVERY KID'S GUIDE ~~...~~SONAL POWER

DAT

OCT 2

NOV

AND POSITIVE SELF-ESTEEM

Gershen Kaufman, Ph.D.,
Lev Raphael, Ph.D., and Pamela Espeland

free spirit
PUBLISHING®

Works
for kids®

Library of Congress Cataloging-in-Publication Data

Kaufman, Gershen.
  Stick up for yourself! : every kid's guide to personal power and positive self-esteem / Gershen Kaufman, Lev Raphael, Pamela Espeland.
    p. cm.
  Includes index.
  Summary: Discusses problems facing young people such as making choices, learning about and liking yourself, and solving problems.
  ISBN 1-57542-068-6 (pbk.)
  1. Assertiveness (Psychology)—Juvenile literature. 2. Control (Psychology)—Juvenile literature. 3. Self-esteem—Juvenile literature. [1. Assertiveness (Psychology 2. Self-esteem.] I. Title. II. Raphael, Lev. III. Espeland, Pamela.

BF575.A85 K38 1999
158'.083'4 21—dc21   99-044134

The following are registered trademarks of Free Spirit Publishing Inc.:

FREE SPIRIT®
FREE SPIRIT PUBLISHING®
SELF-HELP FOR TEENS®
SELF-HELP FOR KIDS®
WORKS FOR KIDS®
THE FREE SPIRITED CLASSROOM®

free spirit
PUBLiSHiNG®
Works for kids®

10 9 8 7 6 5 4 3
Printed in the United States of America

Cover design by Percolator
Book design and typesetting by Marieka Heinlen
Illustrations by Harry Pulver Jr.
Index compiled by Eileen Quam

Free Spirit Publishing Inc.
217 Fifth Avenue North, Suite 200
Minneapolis, MN 55401-1299
(612) 338-2068
help4kids@freespirit.com
www.freespirit.com